HARD BOP

HARD BOP

JAZZ AND
BLACK MUSIC
1955-1965

DAVID H. ROSENTHAL

OXFORD UNIVERSITY PRESS
New York   Oxford

Oxford University Press

Oxford   New York   Toronto
Delhi   Bombay   Calcutta   Madras   Karachi
Kuala Lumpur   Singapore   Hong Kong   Tokyo
Nairobi   Dar es Salaam   Cape Town
Melbourne   Auckland   Madrid

and associated companies in
Berlin   Ibadan

Copyright © 1992 by David H. Rosenthal

First published in 1992 by Oxford University Press, Inc.,
198 Madison Avenue, New York, New York 10016-4314

First issued as an Oxford University Press paperback, 1993

Oxford is a registered trademark of Oxford University Press

Library of Congress Cataloging-in-Publication Data
Rosenthal, David, 1945–
Hard bop : jazz and Black music, 1955–1965 / David H. Rosenthal.
p.   cm.
Discography: p.
Includes index.
ISBN 0–19–505869–0
ISBN 0–19–508556–6 (pbk.)
1. Bop (Music)—History and criticism.   2. Jazz—1951–1960—
History and criticism.   3. Jazz—1961–1970—History and criticism.
4. Afro-Americans—Music—History and criticism.   I. Title.
ML3508.R68   1992
781.65′5—dc20   91–15669   CIP   MN

The following page is regarded as an extension of the copyright page.

2 4 6 8 10 9 7 5 3

Printed in the United States of America

for Alan Rosenthal

PREFACE

My brother David was fourteen (I was ten) when he discovered jazz while attending one of those music and art summer camps in the Berkshires. Chuck Israels, soon to be Bill Evans's bassist, was the son of the woman who ran the place. Randy Weston, a fabulous pianist, would drop by to play basketball. Within a year, David knew more about jazz than many adult jazz-lovers ever do (many of the thoughts contained in these pages were already being expressed), and had managed by hook or crook to gather around himself a very serious little record collection.

At this time (1960), almost all the musicians David discusses in this book were hard at work creating sounds that are still lighting fires under jazz enthusiasts. "Hard bop," whatever the hotly-debated merits of the term, was "alive," by which I mean not just that the music was being played (as it still is), but that it was responding with passionate urgency (as it emphatically no longer is) to its own imbedded implications and those of the larger surrounding culture. It was in, of, and about the world in which it lived.

To David, a poet, critic, and savvy observer of the chaotic postwar world, this quality of *currency* was never secondary throughout his thirty-year involvement in jazz. Music was only one of the trouble spots he kept an eye on, and he was untiring—ruthless, really—in his determination to pull it all together. Not a jazz musician but a jazz-loving artist who was very much of like mind, David was the perfect man for the job of chronicling the complex processes by which jazz flowed into and out of its "hip" environs. He especially relished those dizzying moments when some new artistic flowering, individual or collective, would swoop down to startle sleepy expectations.

Conversely, he distrusted art that had been cut off from its own time to drift, encapsulated and revered, into the future. As the last chapters of this book were being completed, it appeared that jazz might be headed for just such a fate. The "nostalgic nineties" were in full swing (more people probably heard John Lennon's "Imagine" in 1991 than during the entire 1970s). The big jazz labels, seeking salvation by promoting a small group of eighteen-to-twenty-five-year-old males as the "young lions" of their generation, had giddily exhumed a number of early-sixties musical, demographic, and sartorial clichés. Lincoln Center launched a successful jazz program, while previously all-classical magazines and record outlets expanded their well-guarded boundaries just far enough to include jazz. Such intimations of respectability made it seem that "standard repertoire" classical music and 1945–1970 jazz were preparing to share a single high-toned niche in the twenty-first century.

David was disheartened by such possibilities. We spent many hours brooding together over the post-apocalyptic state of our beloved culture, a state he once likened to a garbage can that had been overturned on a windy day. As jazz musicians and listeners continually readjust their fix on the music's future, strength and sanity can be derived from David's refusal to "dumb down" the past in terms of later developments. It was utterly characteristic of him to write (in Chapter 3), "Jazz has always been a volatile music, changing quickly and often, and the hard-bop period . . . represents a moment of balance and polish in the work of many musicians. . . . (But) the elegant equilibriums thus achieved cannot be sustained for long. Such styles generate their own pressures for radical change." No one would cite the jazz of the last fifteen years as a shining example of healthy evolution; David's use of the present tense in this passage typifies his uncompromising attitude.

David completed the writing of this book in 1990. Although he continued following the jazz scene after that, his views on the music discussed here, molded by a lifetime of intense concentration, remained about the same. The major exception to this was the pianist Elmo Hope. In 1991, Blue Note reissued Hope's two ten-inch LPs, from 1953 and 1954, on CD. David was struck by the strength, focus, and originality of the 1953 trio date (with Percy Heath on bass and Philly Joe Jones on drums). He felt that he had been too dismissive of Hope's pre-1959 playing, and realized that inadequate rehearsal opportunities and the exigencies of heroin had conspired to misrepresent Hope as much more of a "late bloomer" than he really was. Many of the qualities David described in Hope's Hifijazz and Riverside albums can be heard to only slightly less stunning effect on this wonderful earlier session.

Finally, a personal note. Although David and I certainly had our differences in musical outlook, there is no point in pretending otherwise: his view of the jazz universe, the thoughts contained in these pages, were the mother's milk that started and guided me in my life as a jazz pianist. As my family continues struggling with the emptiness left by his unexpected illness and death, this "piece" of him, recalling so powerfully the smoke-filled, jazz-filled hours we spent together, is a tremendous comfort.

Alan Rosenthal
April 28, 1993

CONTENTS

HARD BOP

INTRODUCTION

In January 1972, in a scene straight out of "Frankie and
Johnny," trumpeter Lee Morgan was shot dead by his mistress
at Slug's, a jazz club on New York City's Lower East Side.
Morgan was thirty-three years old. His death—spectacular in
jazz not so much because he was young as because it involved a
woman instead of drugs—is remembered thus by one of his
closest musical associates: "For years Lee had been with Helen
[More], an older woman—maybe ten years older than him—
who sort of looked after him and had straightened him out a
little, helped him stay away from dope. A few weeks before his
death, Lee had started hanging out with a younger girl, very
pretty; she looked like Angela Davis. He was taking her all
over town, showing her off to his friends. One day he dropped
by the school in Harlem where I was teaching jazz workshops
and introduced her to all of us.

"That night in January was one of the coldest nights of the
year. It was about five degrees below zero, and Lee was relaxing
between sets at the bar with this fine new girlfriend of his
when Helen walked in. She came up to him, but Lee didn't
want to be bothered and he walked her over to a table, sat her
down, and told her to wait. Then he went back to the bar. After
a while she came up to him again. This time Lee took her by

3

the shoulders and, without her overcoat or anything, marched her over to the door and put her out in the cold. Now she had Lee's pistol in her pocketbook, and when she came back in she pulled it out and shot him: one of those shots that go straight to the heart. A little red stain came up on his shirt—the bleeding was all inside—and a few minutes later he was dead. Then she realized what had happened and she was crying and hanging over him and screaming 'Mogie'—that was what she called him—'What have I done?' But he was dead."*

In a number of respects, Morgan could be considered a quintessential—or even *the* quintessential—hard bopper. His sardonic, "dirty" solos, full of aggressively bent, half-valved, and smeared notes, epitomized the "badness" many jazzmen of his school strove to achieve. Like James Brown in soul music, he had honed his time, attack, and timbre to razor sharpness. The development of his style, from its early bebop-influenced phase when he was with Dizzy Gillespie's big band to the surging modal compositions of his later records, closely paralleled hard bop's evolution. Morgan's life and personality—the moody arrogance that still glares out at us from so many photos, and his readiness to live willfully for the moment—were also those of a typical jazz hipster of the era. Finally, his death coincided with the collapse of hard bop artistically and economically (as music with a large enough audience to support it). And, of course, it deprived the school of its star trumpet player.

Morgan grew up in North Philadelphia, coming of age at a time when black neighborhoods in America's big cities pulsed with the sounds of jazz and virtually every block was home to at least a few knowledgeable jazz fans. One such fan was Lee's older sister Ernestine, who—in addition to playing the piano and organ—took charge of her brother's musical education. When Lee was ten or twelve, she brought him along with her to hear such eminent beboppers as Charlie Parker and Bud Powell

* All citations without references are based on the author's interviews.

at the Earle Theatre. At the age of fourteen, Lee got his first trumpet: a gift from Ernestine. He attended high school at Mastbaum Tech, which, like Cass Tech in Detroit and Du Sable in Chicago, was a hotbed of adolescent jazz musicians, many of them stars-to-be. At fifteen, Lee formed a band with other teenagers that began playing local dances and whose personnel included, at various times, pianist Bobby Timmons, bassists Henry Grimes and Spanky DeBrest, and drummers Lex Humphries and Albert "Tootie" Heath. He also sat in at the Music City instrument shop's "workshop sessions" with drummers Art Blakey, Kenny Clarke, and Max Roach; saxophonists Sonny Stitt and Sonny Rollins; trumpeters Miles Davis, Kenny Dorham, Roy Eldridge, and Dizzy Gillespie; and pianist Bud Powell.

The ferment of Philly's jazz scene and Lee's place in it were recently recalled by bassist Reggie Workman: "Lee grew up in North Philadelphia, a poor neighborhood with a mixture of working-class people. Some were doing okay, some weren't. Lee was like a child prodigy, but there were many of them in Philadelphia at that time, including his friend Kenny Rodgers, who played alto sax. He and Kenny were the stars at Mastbaum Tech. Lee was very well-disciplined. Very jovial, with a great sense of humor—an almost exaggerated sense of humor. He was from a very close-knit family. His older sister [Ernestine] was great friends with my older sister Gloria. They were in a choir together—a community choir. But you have peer pressure in communities like that. The *real* music of that day was jazz: Charlie Parker, Percy Heath, people like that.

"Lee came up when Philly jazz was very strong and there were lots of clubs: Pep's, the Showboat, the Blue Note around 15th and Ridge, the Oasis, the Aqua Lounge in West Philly, plus all kinds of social clubs and taverns that had live music. The owners and managers were so into music that they'd allow us to have jam sessions and come into the clubs and play during the early evening hours, even though we were too young to drink. There was a very healthy music scene in the community taverns at that time, aside from the fact that there were people like Tommy Monroe who ran music workshops for young musicians, or Owen Marshall's big band workshop with new music he wrote and that rehearsed in living rooms, taverns, ballrooms, any place that had a piano and chairs and where we could make music. [Rodgers's alto playing and some of Marshall's compositions can be heard on *Lee Morgan Sextet*, Blue Note.]

"Lee worked very hard at his craft and understood the oral tradition of jazz. He had an incredible record library and all of us would get together every week to listen to his records. His parents helped him out with that, and he used to also go out and hustle and work to get those records. We'd listen to records for hours at a time at his place. He was sought after at a very young age to *leave* Philadelphia because people would hear him at Music City, where we'd have workshops with Blakey, Coltrane, Jimmy Heath, Herbie Nichols, whoever was in town. His parents always supported his interest in music. Now Kenny Rodgers was very advanced too, but he didn't move into the music business because he got married at a young age. Some of the others in our crowd were Donald Wilson [trumpet and piano], Stanley Wilson [tenor sax], Owen Marshall, Johnny Splawn [trumpet], James (Spanky) DeBrest, and McCoy Tyner. They came in waves. Lee and I and the Wilson brothers were all in one age bracket. Philadelphia wasn't unique in that sense. Chicago and Detroit were like that too—any place where there were factories and parents migrating for jobs. A lot stopped in Philadelphia because New York wasn't so comfortable and it was easier to settle down in Philly.

"Lee was a very sensitive human being. He'd reach out and help anyone he felt had merit, and he helped a lot of us to make it in music. He was very, very cocky, very childlike, and very arrogant in his own way. He was always searching for new vistas, comparing notes and telling us about his experiences when he'd come back to Philadelphia. He *loved* Fats Navarro. He knew about everybody from Pops [Louis Armstrong] right on up to today, yet he amalgamated it all into his own sound so you knew right away it was him playing."

In 1956—all of eighteen years old—Morgan cut his first records as a leader for Blue Note and Savoy (two of the era's four main New York–based independent jazz labels, the others being Prestige and Riverside) and toured, first with Art Blakey's Jazz Messengers and then with Dizzy Gillespie's orchestra. Nat Hentoff, in his liner notes for Morgan's *Leeway* album, described the impact of his first exposure to Dizzy's protégé: "Every listener to jazz has had a few experiences so startling that they are literally unforgettable. One of mine took place during an engagement the Dizzy Gillespie big band had at Birdland in 1957. My back was to the bandstand as the band started 'Night in Tunisia.' Suddenly, a trumpet soared out of the band into a break that was so vividly brilliant and electrifying that all conversation in the room stopped and those of us who were gesturing were frozen with hands outstretched. After the first thunderclap impact, I turned and saw that the trumpeter was the very young sideman from Philadelphia, Lee Morgan." When the Gillespie big band disbanded in 1958, Lee rejoined the Jazz Messengers, with whom he played until 1961 and again from 1964 to 1966.

It was during these years that Morgan evolved into a major jazz stylist. His early playing, though impressive both for its technical mastery and for its bravado, betrayed the not entirely assimilated influences of his favorite trumpeters: Fats Navarro, Clifford Brown, Dizzy Gillespie, Miles Davis, and Kenny Dorham (in descending order of importance by Lee's own ranking). This order is by no means casual, for Morgan's early affinities were clearly more with the "extroverted" school represented by the first three than with Davis's or Dorham's lyrical and pensive styles. With the passage of time and perhaps under Blakey's tutelage, Morgan's solos became more melodic: he played fewer notes, and they counted more. His tone darkened, losing much of its effervescent, Clifford Brown–like sweetness and acquiring a timbre that seemed to convey a mixture of bitter irony and sorrow. Though—like hard bop itself—Morgan's style remained rooted in the bebop idiom, by 1960 he had developed an unmistakable sound, attack, and phrasing that fit in perfectly with Wayne Shorter's brass anthems and with the spirit of the Jazz Messengers as a whole, at once sinister and exuberant.

In 1964, Morgan had a hit in "The Sidewinder," a rolling, punching blues with a heavy R & B beat that took his disc of the same name to number twenty-five on *Billboard*'s LP charts. The song was widely played on the radio and in 1965 even cropped up (with strings) as background music for a Chrysler television commercial. Despite several efforts—for example, "The Rumproller" and "Cornbread"—Morgan was never able to repeat this success. And in fact, within only a few years of his triumph, jazz had lost most of its popularity among both blacks and whites, and musicians of his sort were viewed as anachronisms by listeners attuned to Motown and rock. Morgan had hit the scene during the last period in which jazz customarily attracted the hippest young black musicians: the most musically advanced, with the solidest technical skills and the strongest sense of themselves not only as entertainers but as artists. By 1970 this scene was fading fast, while the network of independent jazz record labels, black dj's, and distributors that had nurtured and sometimes exploited it was rapidly disintegrating. Working- and middle-class blacks, fleeing escalating street crime and riots and encouraged by laws forbidding housing discrimination, forsook neighborhoods that had just recently seethed with musical activity—a world of jazz and blues, R & B, aspiring doo-woppers crooning on street corners, gospel, and, of course, families for whom singing and playing were part of everyday life. They left behind smoldering ruins and an underclass that would henceforth be left to its own devices.

Morgan, because of his work with the Jazz Messengers and his success with "The Sidewinder," remained popular enough to make a living playing jazz. But many others of his generation had to abandon their music or water it down in a quest for commercial success or, in some cases, mere survival. While remaining true to jazz, Morgan's own records deteriorated in the late sixties and early seventies. He seemed to be turning into a mannerist of his own style, repeating his clichés without the conviction and sense of discovery that had made his earlier LPs and live performances so riveting. In short, he was in a rut, while the milieu that had buoyed him up—ghetto life with jazz at its center—had vanished.

The decade in which he played such a major role is now just a set of recollections for some and part of "history" for others. Nevertheless, it remains unrivaled for the number of outstanding jazz records it produced. Indeed, to many listeners, hard bop and jazz are still virtually synonymous. When most fans think of jazz, they think of hard bop's mixture of hip street attitudes and a kind of hard-boiled melancholy; and a large percentage of the "new releases" in record stores today are reissues of sides cut during the late fifties and early sixties. To understand this era of extraordinary musical abundance, however, we must first backtrack and consider the meaning and impact of bebop, which laid the foundation for the school and even supplied half its name.

BEBOP

Perhaps the most often-told story in modern-jazz lore is "How Bebop Was Born at Minton's Playhouse." Opened on New York City's 118th Street in 1940, Minton's soon featured a house band led by drummer Kenny Clarke and including pianist Thelonious Monk, trumpeter Joe Guy, and bassist Nick Fenton. Under the management of ex-bandleader Teddy Hill, the club evolved into a musicians' hangout and a focal point for experimentation, drawing advanced Swing musicians like saxophonists Ben Webster and Don Byas, guitarist Charlie Christian, and bassist Jimmy Blanton, along with such incipient beboppers as trumpeter Dizzy Gillespie and pianist Bud Powell. Altoist Charlie Parker also dropped in whenever he was in town. Minton's late-night jam sessions drew some of the best and some of the worst. The latter, however, would "feel a breeze" after a chorus or so. Indeed, another often-told tale about the birth of bebop holds that its "weird" chord changes and keys were designed to hustle incompetent musicians off the stand.

Some of the chaos and excitement of those wild times at Minton's comes through in saxophonist Illinois Jacquet's description of the club in *To Be or Not to Bop*, Dizzy Gillespie's autobiography: "During the time in the forties when Minton's

10

was operating, we used to go up there and jam. I was with the bands at the time, and I would come in and out of town. When I was in the city, we were appearing at the Apollo or downtown at the Paramount or the Strand. After the last show we'd go to Minton's and sit in or listen to some of the guys play.

"It was sorta like a free-for-all. People that could play would wanna sit in. They could get up and play. Take a chorus or join the session. Sometimes there would be guys that couldn't play as well as some of the other guys. Still, they had the opportunity to get up there and play. But sometimes they would be a little off key. They would think that Monk would be in the key of B-flat, and he would be in the key of F-sharp or D natural. And then these guys wouldn't stay on the stand too long because they could never find the keys that Monk was playing in. So right there he knew that they would probably not be qualified to take up all that time with those long undesirable solos. And like Monk and the others would get into some weird keys sometimes, and while they'd be changing keys, things would be getting modern all the time, because the keys were sorta hanging *them* up a little bit too sometimes. But a lotta guys just wanted to get up there and pose, and the music was not coming out; quite naturally they tried to get into another key when they saw them coming. You'd modulate into another key, and they wouldn't stay up there *too* long. Then when they disappeared, the regular guys would come up that could really play, and they'd go on and finish what they were trying to do. So, like, you would get a chance to play things that you would ordinarily play in B-flat, in D natural, see. But you were schooled enough to play in those keys because you knew when you were in a different key.

"There were many, many giants that would come in there to play. People like Dizzy, Charlie Parker, Denzil Best, Harold West, Shadow Wilson. Sometimes the late Sid Catlett would come in. Monk, Sir Charles Thompson, Bud Powell, Freddie Webster, Don Byas. It was just like a jam, somewhere to go and play. Late at night, because it seemed like the music would sound better that time of morning. They didn't have nothing to do but go to bed. They didn't have to make no shows or be between shows. The job was over."[1]

By 1945, the more adventurous among this crew had developed a style—"bop" or "bebop"—that clearly distinguished them from their elders. Its leading lights (some were already beboppers in 1945; others emerged over the next few years) were trumpeters Gillespie, Fats Navarro, Miles Davis, and Kenny Dorham; saxophonists Parker, Sonny Stitt, and Dexter Gordon; pianists Monk and Bud Powell; drummers Clarke, Max Roach, and Art Blakey; and composer Tadd Dameron. Technically, bebop was characterized by fast tempos, complex harmonies, intricate melodies, and rhythm sections that laid down a steady beat only on the bass and the drummer's ride cymbal. Bebop tunes were often labyrinthine, full of surprising twists and turns. All these factors—plus the predominance of small combos in bebop—set the music apart from the Swing bands of the 1930s.

As a style, bebop was remarkably of a piece, best played by the nucleus of musicians who had been responsible for its technical and aesthetic breakthroughs. Because of the school's compactness, many if not most bebop tunes are also "typical" ones. For instance, Charlie Parker's composition "Donna Lee," which he recorded for Savoy Records with Miles Davis, Bud Powell, bassist Tommy Potter, and Max Roach, is based on the chords to the popular song "Indiana." This in itself was a standard bebop procedure, and "Donna Lee" is a classic bebop melody: serpentine, eccentrically syncopated, and based more on improvisational phrasing than on a simple, "songlike" theme. The three soloists (Parker, Davis, and Powell) all play long phrases that frequently violate the bar lines, spilling over them and beginning and ending in unexpected places. These phrases are counterbalanced, especially in Parker's solo, by fragmentary shorter ones: scraps of material that add to the performance's impromptu quality and to the feeling that we're listening to someone "think aloud," trying out motifs as he modulates from one idea to another. The dense rhythmic counterpoint is enriched by Powell's and, even more, Roach's use of accents placed asymmetrically, sometimes in response to the solos but often tugging against them. Harmonically, all three statements are full of "passing" notes and forays into the outer reaches of the chords. Finally, Parker's tone, slightly shrill, hard-edged, vibratoless and glossy, also tells us we're listening to bebop. Indeed, it formed the basis for virtually every black jazz altoist's sound between 1945 and 1960. On "Donna Lee" and dozens of other masterpieces of the era, everything is off center, almost perversely so . . . *eppur si muove!* (Galileo's words: "And yet it moves!") The most intricate acrobatics are accomplished with apparently effortless grace and swing.

More than forty years later, bebop's innovations have been thoroughly absorbed into jazz. Bebop was, after all, a form of *jazz*, and it was also a logical and inevitable extension of what had come before it. Nonetheless, its initial appearance struck young musicians like a bolt of lightning. Ross Russell, in his novel *The Sound*, evokes one variant of this response: "The music was full of splintered phrasing and astringent sounds. Its rhythm was angular and complex, queer, off center, yet riveted to some atavistic rock. After a few bars it began to eat away at the nervous system, like something one might have heard at a tribal dance in Africa. It hypnotized. At the same time it irritated. It was jazz. Yet it was not jazz. Certainly it had little in common with the music of Ellington and Goodman, or the swing style that Bernie [the book's hero, a white pianist] understood. It seemed to reflect the turmoil and insecurity of the war years. At the same time it implied a profound contempt for those who had been foolish enough to become involved with the war. But it came forth full loined and girded, arrogant and disquieting. Quite unmistakably, it was all of a piece. Bernie listened and made mental notes. Harmonically the style had not advanced much beyond Ravel and French impressionism. The unique aspects lay rather in the airy,

vibratoless intonation of the instruments, more in the classical style than jazz, and in the dodging, off-center rhythms. This
could all be reduced fairly to notation, scored and arranged, and
might very well decribe the form, but would it explain the
emotional content? Bernie wondered how it had all come
about and if the girl had the wit or the will to tell him, and, if
so, in what sort of language that he might understand. *Cool!*
Gone! Even, the *greatest*—none of these seemed adequate or
precise. The set came to a close. House lights came up. There
was no mistaking the reaction of the crowd. The room began to
buzz with muted, excited conversation."[2]

As this passage suggests, it was not just bebop's technical
side but also its emotional charge and even the "hip" world
that surrounded it that were so striking and seductive. The
United States was entering a period of anesthetized consumer-
ism in 1945, but important minorities either opted out of or
were forcibly excluded from these values. In another passage in
the same novel, Russell describes bebop's audience: "In addition to the 'young dancing crowd,' Jimmy Vann [leader of the
big band in which Bernie plays] was drawing from another
group unique in music history. Bernie could well remember
the 'alligators' of the late swing period, those serious types,
self-styled students of American jazz, who used to edge up to
the orchestra shell and remain there all night, indefatigably
listening. The 'alligators' were timid souls and few in number.
Bernie wondered if they were the spiritual fathers of the new
hipster hordes. Certainly the audience of pure listeners, as
distinguished from those who came merely to dance, had
undergone a remarkable expansion . . . They were most numerous in and around San Francisco. They paid their way into
the dance halls. No question there! But all spending stopped
at the box office. They formed a cordon several ranks deep
around the orchestra shell, cutting dancers off from the source
of the music. They ducked under trombone slides, jostled
Hassan's drums and sometimes Bernie's piano bench. They did
not date. This was considered corny. They did not drink. Also

corny. They gave the impression that they had never danced a step in their lives, nor had any intention of so doing. They closed around the bandstand like a cordon of police protecting a head of state . . .

"Between sets they would gravitate to the roped-off section of tables usually found in the Western dance halls and there, among the litter of iced coffee glasses, and a haze of smoke, laced with the sweet pungent aroma of freshly-burned marijuana, establish their headquarters."[3]

Bebop, of course, was many things to many people. To some it was a fad, a weird style of dressing and talking. An ad for Fox Bros. Tailors in Chicago featured the following spiel: "That's right, man! Bop King, Dizzy Gillespie and his great band are another addition to the steadily growing number of top musicians who have made the switch to FOX BROS. for the greatest uniforms and accessories. You dig?" The ad then gives Fox Bros.' prices for "bop ties," "bop caps," and "bop crushers," and ends by urging customers to "order YOUR Leopard Skin Jacket as worn by Dizzy Gillespie . . . BOP IN AND LET FOX BUILD YOU A CRAZY BOX!"[4]

To young beboppers, the new music was a banner of rebellion, filled with the excitement of discovery, turning jazz inside out and electrifying a musical language in danger of excessive codification. To "hipsters" it was an alternative lifestyle, pursued with varying degrees of fanaticism. At its most extreme, the world of bebop meant rejecting respectability in favor of a bohemian quest for strong sensations, for the aesthetic and spiritual. Through their dress, vaguely suggestive of European literary intellectuals—berets, goatees, horn-rimmed glasses—beboppers and their followers clearly signaled their affinities.

In *Blues People*, an excellent study of the sociology of jazz, Leroi Jones (Amiri Baraka) points to bebop's obvious connection with frustrated black hopes: that the masses moving north during World War II would encounter an integrated society, and that soldiers risking their lives for "democracy" would find justice on their return home. The resulting fury and greater cultural sophistication among urban blacks were certainly two of the vectors converging in bebop: "The Negro music that developed in the forties had more than an accidental implication of social upheaval associated with it. To a certain extent, the music resulted from conscious attempts to remove it from the danger of mainstream dilution or even understanding. For one thing, the young musicians began to think of themselves as *serious* musicians, even artists, and not performers. And that attitude erased immediately the protective and parochial atmosphere of 'the folk expression' from jazz. Musicians like Charlie Parker, Thelonious Monk, and Dizzy Gillespie were all quoted at various times as saying, 'I don't care if you listen to my music or not.' This attitude certainly must have mystified the speakeasy–Charleston–Cotton-Club set of white Americans, who had identified jazz only with liberation from the social responsibilities of full ctitzenship."[5]

Bebop, then, was partly an outburst of black rage and denial, an attempt to create an alternative world from which one could gaze with distant irony at "square" America. As a bohemian subculture, it was far more tumultuous and original, more genuinely homegrown, than such relatively respectable predecessors as the "Harlem Renaissance" of the 1920s. Cool, ironic distance; it's not for nothing that beboppers' favorite drug was heroin. In the late 1940s, having made a decision familiar to anyone who's watched *The Godfather*, the Mafia introduced heroin into black ghettos in New York and other cities. The drug's impact on musicians was devastating. Of course, no one forced them to take it, and some didn't, at least not very often—for example, Gillespie, Monk, and vibist Milt Jackson. On the other hand, for "keeping cool" in the face of humiliating and exasperating circumstances, heroin is remarkably effective. In addition to being black, beboppers also had to cope with a sense of being undervalued as artists, denied respect and recognition, and forced to create under sordid and exploitative conditions. Whether all these feelings were equally justified is perhaps debatable, but they have been the common ones among modern-jazz musicians. A list of some major trumpeters of the late 1940s should suggest the extent of heroin addiction—and its consequences—among beboppers: Miles Davis (drug problems in the early 1950s); Freddie Webster (dead at thirty in 1947, a "legendary" figure who scarcely recorded, the Buddy Bolden of modern jazz); Little Benny Harris (best known as composer of "Ornithology," rarely recorded); Sonny Berman (dead at twenty-three in 1947); Red Rodney and Howard McGhee (both out of commission during much of the 1950s); and Fats Navarro (dead in 1950 at twenty-six of tuberculosis complicated by drug addiction).

Most of these musicians were black (the exceptions being Berman and Rodney), as were all the most original and influential beboppers. Many of the bands and the scene surrounding the music, however, were racially mixed. Where bebop was performed in New York City says a lot about the pigmentation of its audience. Some of the best clubs were in Harlem and Bedford Stuyvesant; others were in Greenwich Village, an island of at least partial integration though predominantly white. The movement's epicenter, however, was 52nd Street between 5th and 6th avenues, in the heart of midtown Manhattan. This block, known simply as "The Street," housed clubs like the 3 Deuces, the Downbeat, the Famous Door, the Spotlite, Kelly's Stables, the Yacht Club, and the Onyx. In Ira Gitler's survey of bebop, *Jazz Masters of the 40s,* Dexter Gordon sums up what many musicians felt about The Street: "Unquestionably, it was the most exciting half a block in the world. Everything was going on—music, chicks, connections . . . so many musicians working down there, side by side."6

From 1945 till the mid-sixties, jazz was also the preferred music of white renegades, bohemians, and artists. It was particularly central for the loose-knit group of writers associated with the "beat" movement. Jack Kerouac, for example, declared that it all began for him when saxophonist Lester Young turned him on in 1941 to his first joint of marijuana at Minton's. Allen Ginsberg's most celebrated poem, "Howl," begins with these lines:

> I saw the best minds of my generation destroyed by madness,
>   starving hysterical naked,
> dragging themselves through the negro streets at dawn
>   looking for an angry fix,
> angelheaded hipsters burning for the ancient heavenly
>   connection to the starry dynamo in the machinery of
>   night,
> who poverty and tatters and hollow-eyed and high sat up
>   smoking in the supernatural darkness of cold-water flats
> floating across the tops of cities contemplating jazz,[7]

Although "Howl" is not *about* jazz, jazz enters the poem in a number of guises and plays a number of roles in it. In these lines and elsewhere, jazz is dangled like a talisman. It has the power to evoke worlds of desolate courage. It lives by its improvisatory risk-taking and exploration of what came to be known literarily as "open form." And it "fits" with the poem's preceding imagery of drugs, ghettos, transcendence-out-of-squalor, and, of course, rebellion and rejection of bourgeois complacency. Bebop and jazz as a whole, for obvious reasons, could not *mean* the same things to whites as they did to blacks. Nonetheless, the implications and significances ascribed to them in "Howl" are not very different from those we find in black poet Amiri Baraka's work in the 1950s.

Yet despite all these associations and bebop's experimental audacity, feelings of rage and rebelliousness do not come through in the music itself. Most bebop, in fact, is exuberant, and this is not primarily a matter of fast tempos. The joy of creation and delight in newness are its most notable affects, and in many bebop performances, it would be hard to identify any other, more nonmusical emotion being expressed. Two exceptions, and for this reason two artists whose work foreshadowed hard bop's evolution in the 1950s, were Tadd Dameron and Bud Powell.

If Charlie Parker was bebop's improvisational genius, its Louis Armstrong, then Dameron (1917–1965)—all other things being equal—would have been its Duke Ellington. All other things, however, were not equal. Dameron's career was repeatedly thrown off track by heroin addiction, and he suffered an enforced stay at the Federal Narcotics Hospital in Lexington, Kentucky, from 1958 to 1961. Though there is enough Dameron on records to demonstrate his brilliance, he did not bequeath anything like the corpus Ellington did; nor, except for a period in the late forties, could he keep a regular working band together.

Dameron's genius lay in his gift for truly memorable melodies, simple yet full of freshness and surprise, songlike and meshed with the harmonies that underpinned them in a way characteristic of the best twentieth-century North American pop and jazz composers. Not surprisingly, Dameron's two heroes were George Gershwin and Duke Ellington. In a conversation with Ira Gitler, he remarked: "When I heard George Gershwin, then I said, 'This is really it.' Gershwin was beautiful. Gershwin and Duke Ellington—always Duke Ellington."[8] Gitler has also quoted Dameron on his general approach to music: "Standing in front of his band while rehearsing for a recording date in 1953, he told his men: 'Make those phrases flow. When I write something it's with beauty in mind. It has to swing, sure, but it has to be beautiful.' In 1961 he told me, 'I'm trying to stress melody, with flowing chords, chords that make the melody interesting. I'm trying to build a bridge between popular music and the so-called modern music. I think there is too wide a gap. You can tell that from the way they sell.'"[9]

What this bridge was constructed of can be heard on recordings like Dizzy Gillespie's 1946 version of "Our Delight." The tune, like a number of Dameron's compositions, has entered the standard jazz repertoire and is typical of his best work. In some ways closer to Swing tunes than to improvisation-based lines like "Donna Lee," "Our Delight" is a genuine *song:* a bubbly, jaggedly ascending theme that sticks in one's mind, enriched by harmonic interplay between a flaming trumpet section led by Dizzy; creamy, moaning reeds; and crooning trombones. The written accompaniments to the solos—in particular the leader's two statements—are also full of inventiveness, creating call-and-response patterns and countermelodies. What is boppish here is the off-center, syncopated melody, as well as the shifting, internal voicings of the chords, especially at the very end. These voicings, along with a love of tuneful melodies that one walks out of a jazz club humming, were Tadd's main legacy to such composers and arrangers as Benny Golson, Gigi Gryce, and Jimmy Heath.

     While the joy and beauty of Dameron's work belied his hard life, Bud Powell (1924–1966) created a music in which anguish and demoniacal fury alternated and at times mingled. From the late forties on, Powell was in and out of mental hospitals, undergoing shock treatments and suffering a series of psychotic episodes. Even when more or less functional, Powell was known as a sullen and eccentric character. Liquor aggravated his problems, sometimes causing him to "flip out" with unpredictable consequences. Chronic liver disease and tuberculosis also plagued him in the latter part of his life.

     With a few exceptions (most notably *The Scene Changes,* an album he cut for Blue Note Records in 1959), Powell's best recorded work dates from the 1945–1953 period. During those years he was the unchallenged king of bebop piano, with a status analogous to Charlie Parker's on alto saxophone. Most hip young pianists aspired to play like Bud, and his influence, though diluted, continues to be felt today. Like Bird (Parker), Bud could solo at breathtaking speeds yet retain a lucidity and precision in accentuation, an ability to *think* in fifth gear, that are beyond most musicians.

     Although Bud recorded with virtually all the major bebop-

pers—Parker, Gillespie, Gordon, Navarro, Stitt, and others—
most of the real depths and heights of his work are found on his
trio and solo performances. On "Tempus Fugit," for example
(recorded for Verve in 1949 with bassist Ray Brown and Max
Roach), torment and frenzy come together in the theme, an up-
tempo minor original whose portentous rolling chords punctu-
ate a whiplike, forward-driven melody. Bud's solo is a torrent
of notes, which at first flow forth in smooth, legato phrases but
which build in percussive ferocity as he hammers out transposed and repeated phrases and descending runs. Roach's
insistent accentuation and Powell's own restlessly prodding
left hand add to the urgency until Powell takes the theme out,
playing faster and striking the notes harder this time.

"Tempus Fugit" is vintage bebop, to be sure, yet there's
something else present, something suggestive of jazz in the
fifties. The minor mode in itself makes the piece somewhat
unusual in bebop and accounts for part of the tune's dark
mood. This quality, however, derives mainly from Bud's solo.
Equally far from the exuberance we hear in Parker and Gillespie and from Dameron's lush romanticism, Bud's playing is
full of seething intensity, and it is this brooding, obsessive side
of Powell that leads into hard bop.

All the musicians comprising bebop's first wave had come
up through Swing: Parker had played with Jay McShann,
Powell with Cootie Williams, Gillespie with Cab Calloway,
Monk with Coleman Hawkins, and Navarro with Andy Kirk.
Tadd Dameron wrote two of his most popular tunes, "Good
Bait" and "Stay on It," for Count Basie's orchestra. In the late
1940s, however, the first generation primarily *formed* by
bebop—those who had been fifteen or younger in 1945—began
to emerge. For these youngsters, modern jazz was necessarily a
point of departure, a language they had inherited and in which
they had to find something new to say.

Although groups of second-wave beboppers sprang up in all
big North American cities, those who attracted attention first
were New Yorkers like saxophonists Sonny Rollins and Jackie

McLean, pianist Kenny Drew, and drummer Art Taylor, all of whom lived in Harlem. Such teenagers were eager apprentices, striving to emulate not just bebop as music but also hip talk, hip dress, and often hip drugs—that is, heroin. Harlem had a vigorous jazz scene, including clubs like Minton's, Club Lido, Monroe's Uptown House, the Showman Bar, Club Harlem, Small's Paradise, Connie's Inn, the Baby Grand; the Apollo Theatre; and the Audubon and Renaissance ballrooms. Since New York City was home to most beboppers, these young musicians had plenty of chances to rub elbows with their idols. McLean, for instance, was befriended and informally taught by Charlie Parker, Bud Powell, and Thelonious Monk. One of his first professional gigs was with Monk's band.

Jackie was also closely involved in the late forties and early fifties with Miles Davis, who in a sense was the first second-wave bebopper, since almost from the beginning he had worked with groups like Billy Eckstine's bebop big band and Charlie Parker's quintet. It is perhaps significant that while musicians like Gillespie and Powell remained essentially be-boppers in the fifties and sixties Davis played a key role in most jazz styles *after* bebop, nor would anyone think of citing his work between 1945 and 1950 as the best he has done.

Both McLean and Rollins began playing professionally in their teens, often at dances and "cocktail sips" in Harlem but also on gigs with Monk, Powell, and the like. McLean's early playing, of which our first recorded example is Davis's *Dig* session (with Rollins, pianist Walter Bishop, Jr., Tommy Potter, and Art Blakey), is particularly intriguing and suggestive of the shape of jazz to come. On the title cut, one can hear all his defects at the age of nineteen. His solo is stiff, full of meaningless runs, strange pauses as though he were trying to think of what to play next, and reheated Charlie Parker licks all thrown together in disarray. And yet, there's something about his time, his timbre, his way of attacking a note that is riveting. A true cry from the heart, piercing and ragged, McLean's tone has always been his strong point. A mediocre bebopper, he would go on to become a major presence on the hard bop scene, where his ability to create *moods* would count for more than his failure to live up to bebop's standards of quicksilvery inventiveness. (Only in the early sixties would McLean's musical *thinking* mature.)

By 1950, bebop had burnt itself out as a fad and to some extent as a school of jazz, though this statement requires considerable qualification. (After all, many of those who survived the forties—for example, Dizzy, Monk, J.J. Johnson, Kenny Dorham, and Milt Jackson—went on to produce work at least as good in the fifties.) Still, a music that had depended so much on surprise couldn't go on repeating itself. In addition, a new school, "cool jazz," had arisen, dominated by musicians like saxophonists Stan Getz, Lee Konitz, and Gerry Mulligan and pianist Lennie Tristano. Although some blacks—for example, Miles Davis and pianist John Lewis—were involved, at least briefly, with the "cool" movement, it was overwhelmingly a white phenomenon, both in its protagonists and its audience.

Some cool jazz has stood the passage of time very well. Stan Getz's early recordings, for instance, are full of passion, combined with a supple rhythmic sense and a delight in flowing improvisations. Tristano's work, at once cerebral and relentlessly expressive, remains some of the most original piano playing in the history of jazz. The movement as a whole, however, produced a great deal of forgettable "chamber jazz" and preciosity of various sorts. In black neighborhoods, cool jazz went virtually unnoticed, while beboppers languished, finding it harder and harder to get jobs. "Musicians," an ad in *Down Beat* warned at the time, "remember today you not only must be able to play, you must be able to do some acting, singing, dancing and also speak lines."[10] And indeed, at the beginning of the fifties Dizzy Gillespie led a combo that featured more "novelty tunes" than jazz and relied more on his sense of humor than his musicianship. J.J. Johnson, bebop's star trombonist, spent the years between 1952 and 1954 working as a blueprint inspector, while Kenny Dorham's employers at the time included Republic Aviation and the Jack Frost sugar refinery in California.

For a while, it was hard to see what the future of black jazz might be. The early fifties saw an extremely dynamic rhythm-and-blues scene take shape, including a succession of brilliant doo-wop combos like the Ravens, the Clovers, and the Orioles: a New Orleans school centering on Fats Domino, Professor Longhair, Shirley and Lee, and others; urban blues of the Muddy Waters and Bobby Bland type; and much else besides. This music, and not cool jazz, was what chronologically separated bebop and hard bop in ghettos. Young jazz musicians, of course, enjoyed and listened to these R & B sounds which, among other things, began the amalgam of blues and gospel that would later be dubbed "soul music." And it is in this vigorously creative black pop music, at a time when bebop seemed to have lost both its direction and its audience, that some of hard bop's roots may be found.

HARD BOP BEGINS

In an interview with Stanley Crouch, pianist Andrew Hill recalled Chicago's black music scene in the 1950s, when he could "sneak up on a gig with Gene Ammons, play accordion, or back up some rhythm and blues singers like the Flamingos. Then a musician was really getting his music across because there were bars on every corner and you couldn't go anywhere without hearing music. That's why people were so into music. Now they have commodities like ghetto blasters, but they don't have instruments and they don't hear the music. They have become consumers instead of listeners. A consumer buys what he's told to buy. A listener appreciates variety and individuality."[1]

Hill's statement, with its nostalgia for lost worlds of musical bounty, is intriguing on more than one account. Maybe his mentions of the doo-wop group the Flamingos and tenor saxophonist Gene Ammons were casual. On the other hand, both references suggest black music's intersecting variants in the early fifties. The Flamingos are perhaps best known for their version of "I Only Have Eyes for You," a Tin Pan Alley standard whose impact derives from the contrast between a dreamlike, whole-tone-based vamp and a release that explodes into impressionistic chords. As an example of what Ornette

Coleman calls "not-in-tuneness": of subtle and deliberate adjustments of the diatonic scale to create (in this case) an atmosphere of haunting mystery, the recording would be hard to beat. The Flamingos were at once vertebrators of the traditional American songbook, an extension of gospel harmonizing, and pioneers of soul music.

Ammons, likewise, was a musician who could be looked at from several angles. In the 1950s, he cut a series of records for Prestige that featured such astringent hard boppers as John Coltrane, pianist Mal Waldron, and Jackie McLean. Another facet of Ammons—this one closer to Earl Bostic than to McLean—can be heard on his fulsomely romantic rendition of the ballad "My Foolish Heart," which made *Billboard* magazine's black pop charts in 1950.[2] Ammons had also played in Billy Eckstine's 1944–1947 big band alongside such beboppers as Art Blakey, Dexter Gordon, Fats Navarro, and Charlie Parker. At the end of the forties (on the other hand), he replaced Stan Getz in Woody Herman's orchestra, a major incubator of cool jazz. And in the early fifties, "Jug" (as he was called) co-led a two-tenor combo with Sonny Stitt that ripped it up in an area usually defined by jazz critics as "on the border between jazz and R & B."

Leonard Feather's *Encyclopedia of Jazz*, referring both to performances like "My Foolish Heart" and to the Stitt–Ammons duo, declares that Jug "made entry into R & B field with sweet ballad and 'honking' styles before returning to jazz. British critic Alun Morgan said of him, 'Ammons has regained his position as an inventive soloist whose big tone gives him a commanding personality.' "[3] The implication here is that Jug had somehow strayed from the path of righteousness and then returned to it, but in reality he had never *lost* his position as an inventive soloist whose big tone gave him a commanding personality. He had simply played in several contexts—some closer to modern-jazz orthodoxy than others—and in each of them he had remained himself.

Jug's father, as it happened, was Albert Ammons, one of the

finest boogie-woogie pianists. In boogie-woogie's heyday, fewer hairs were split about what was and wasn't "jazz." To some degree, jazz and urban black pop music were coterminous. Bessie Smith, Count Basie, and Albert Ammons were certainly considered part of both. It was only in the late forties—that is, with bebop—that these categories began to diverge more radically. Some musicians accepted the jazz/non-jazz dichotomy; others didn't. Even those who did, however, were often forced to take "non-jazz" gigs. Trumpeter Joe Morris's jump-blues band, for example, included tenor saxophonist Johnny Griffin, trombonist Matthew Gee, pianist Elmo Hope, bassist Percy Heath, and drummer Philly Joe Jones. Some of these musicians may have enjoyed the experience more than others (one suspects that the flamboyant Griffin would have had more fun than the more cerebral and introspective Hope in such a group), but most learned from their R & B experiences and were influenced by them.

Nonetheless, the fact that the jazz–R & B distinction wasn't as clear as some would have made it didn't mean it was nonexistent. The problem in the early fifties was: where do we go from here? Bebop, which had begun as a promise of freedom, had turned into something of a straitjacket, an increasingly codified form of expression. Many of its best practitioners were dead, and others, like Charlie Parker, were in decline. R & B might be a source of new ideas, but it was too limited to satisfy jazz musicians as a regular context. Slowly—hesitantly at first and then more decisively—the outlines of a new, more emotionally expressive and more formally flexible style began to emerge in the music of trumpeters Miles Davis and Clifford Brown, saxophonist Sonny Rollins, pianist Horace Silver, drummer Art Blakey, and others.

Among these, Miles Davis's evolution between 1950 and 1955 was perhaps the most emblematic. Though Miles had been in the bebop movement—and at its very center, with Parker, Dameron, and others—he had never really been *of* it. His spare melodic lines in the middle register and his achingly mournful sound contrasted with the flaming acrobatics of Gillespie, Navarro, and others. Then, in 1949, Davis collaborated with Gil Evans, Lee Konitz, John Lewis, and Gerry Mulligan on what many consider the finest examples of cool jazz (collected by Capitol Records on the LP *Birth of the Cool*). By 1951, Miles's interests had shifted again. In the words of Bob Weinstock, owner of Prestige Records: "Miles sort of disappeared from the scene, and I was on a business trip out to St. Louis, and I knew Miles lived around there. I made some calls, there were a few Davises in the phone book, and I reached his home. They told me he was in Chicago. I said, 'Please, if you should hear from Miles, ask him to call me in New York. I want to record him.' Finally he got in touch with me, and he came back East. Miles, at that time, although he still dug the cool music of Mulligan and Evans, some of the primitiveness in him started to come out. I say primitiveness, because to me the music of the bop masters is primitive music, like the original New Orleans music of King Oliver and Louis. He sort of drifted back into that element, and he liked Sonny Rollins, as crude as Sonny was at that time . . . On his first date, you can hear a very different Miles Davis than on the Capitols."[4]

Over the next few years, Davis recorded infrequently and had other things to think about besides honing his musical conception (he had acquired a heroin habit in 1949 that took him more than four years to break). Nonetheless, the two ten-inch LPs he cut for Blue Note in 1952 and 1953 are fascinating indications of his development. Both feature sextets, whose members include saxophonists Jackie McLean and Jimmy Heath, J.J. Johnson, pianist Gil Coggins, bassist Oscar Pettiford, Art Blakey, and Kenny Clarke. On the one hand, Davis seems to have sloughed off superficial bebop influences. His solos are unadorned (possibly perforce, since one gets the impression that he wasn't practicing much at the time), and his emphasis seems to be on wringing maximum poignancy out of every note. His sound is husky, slightly raspy, and his execution conveys a feeling of tentativeness and vulnerability.

This quality comes across most strongly on ballads like "Yesterdays" and J.J. Johnson's "Enigma," but is also present on up-tempo and medium-tempo numbers. On the other hand, a full third of the twelve tunes (Oscar Pettiford's "Chance It," Ray Brown's and Gil Fuller's "Ray's Idea," "I Waited for You," and "Woody'n You") are either by or associated with Dizzy Gillespie—as if Miles had defiantly set out to show he was so different from Dizzy that he could even play his book without showing the slightest influence.

In many ways, the music on the two dates points ahead to hard bop. There is a marked preference for the minor mode. Up-tempo tunes are the exception. Melodies are simpler and rarely based on bebop's standard chord changes (for example, "I Got Rhythm" and "Indiana"). Above all, the mood of the music is far darker than in bebop. As Leonard Feather remarked in his liner notes: "Davis's solos seem to reflect the complexity of the neurotic world in which we live. The soaring spurts of lyrical exultancy are outnumbered by the somber moment of pensive gloom."

By 1954 Davis had kicked his heroin habit and began recording more frequently, mostly for Prestige Records. Performers on these sessions varied, but the customary rhythm section was Horace Silver, Percy Heath, and Kenny Clarke—one of the most tightly knit and well-balanced trios in jazz history. Their equilibrium came from the contrast between Heath's and Clarke's flowing, cushiony beat and Silver's choppily percussive comping: a mixture of smoothness and roughness that was extraordinarily propulsive. Davis's outstanding record date in 1954, however, featured a group dubbed by Prestige the "Modern Jazz Giants" who, at least on a personal level, worked together in a way that was anything but smooth.

This combo consisted of Davis, Thelonious Monk, Milt Jackson (nicknamed "Bags" because of the circles under his eyes), Heath, and Clarke. They recorded four tunes on December 24, in a session famous in part for the tensions between Monk and Davis. Davis told the pianist to "lay out" (not

accompany his solos). Monk took offense at this order, and one
of their arguments is preserved on wax, with Miles saying,
"Man, you can't start anything" after Monk comes in late on a
theme and Monk instructing the engineer to "put this on the
record—all of it." Miles later told Nat Hentoff: "I love the way
Monk plays and writes, but I can't stand him behind me. He
doesn't give you any support"[5]—a statement, however, that
was not really accurate. Monk was one of the most stimulating
accompanists in jazz, but his notion of "supporting" soloists
included prodding and challenging them. Obviously Davis
wanted someone less demanding and perhaps also someone
with a less forceful personality.

Despite these conflicts, the session produced some of
Davis's best solos ever. One tune, a blues by Jackson entitled
"Bags' Groove," featured two trumpet outings that are remarkable for their economy of means and their extraordinary richness of ideas. Playing few notes, Davis relied on a subtle
rhythmic sense. He could energize a simple phrase by slight
displacements, and he possessed a melodic fecundity that
filled almost every bar with figures that could well be "tunes"
themselves. Davis teaches us what "less is more" means in
jazz. As fellow trumpeter Art Farmer remarked: "When you're
not technically a virtuoso, you have to be saying something.
You've got no place to hide."[6] As a composition, "Bags'
Groove" went on to become a standard at jam sessions. Its
loose-jointed, medium-tempo beat and "catchy" theme made
it a perfect vehicle for both novices and professionals. The
former liked it because it was so easy to play, the latter because
its simplicity forced them to concentrate on musical coherence rather than digital dexterity.

The other important trumpeter to come of age in the early
1950s was Clifford Brown ("Brownie"), who in many ways,
both musically and personally, was the opposite of Davis. If
Davis was the most lunar of modern jazz artists, then Brownie
was the sunniest, with a joyous, bubbly style that overflowed
with high spirits. Born in 1930 in Wilmington, Delaware,

Brownie was performing with beboppers like J.J. Johnson, Max Roach, and Fats Navarro in the late 1940s. Navarro, in particular, both encouraged and influenced him. Another early champion was Dizzy Gillespie. Gillespie visited Brownie in the hospital during his year-long convalescence after an automobile accident in 1950 and urged him to persevere in his career as a trumpeter.

Having recovered from this accident, Brownie worked for two years with Chris Powell's Blue Flames, which, in Ira Gitler's words, "was an R & B unit but in those days bands of that nature had quite a bit of jazz in them."[7] This, Brownie's first extended professional gig, was followed by stints with Tadd Dameron, Lionel Hampton, Art Blakey, and Max Roach. At the time of his death in 1956 in a second road crash—one that also killed Bud Powell's younger brother Richie, a pianist and composer of delicate refinement—Brownie had been co-leading a quintet with Roach for two years.

Today, he is remembered not only for his music but also for his generosity and his determination to avoid the vices that had killed or immobilized so many other jazzmen. Sonny Rollins, who was struggling with some of these vices in the early fifties, told Joe Goldberg that "Clifford was a profound influence on my personal life. He showed me that it was possible to live a good, clean life and still be a good jazz musician."[8] After Clifford's death, Quincy Jones expanded on the point: "Brownie had a very hard job. He constantly struggled to associate jazz, its shepherds, and its sheep, with a cleaner element, and held no room in his heart for bitterness about the publicity-made popularity and success of some of his pseudo-jazz giant brothers, who were sometimes very misleading morally and musically. As a man and a musician, he stood for a perfect example and the rewards of self-discipline."[9]

Perhaps no other modern jazzman was so missed by those who knew him as Clifford Brown. Though he is recalled by some as almost childlike, he was a highly skilled musician—technically one of the best jazz trumpeters who ever lived—as well as a passionate chess player and something of an amateur mathematician. "Clifford always took time to listen to and talk with young people," his widow LaRue wrote recently. "He stressed the need for youngsters, especially aspiring musicians, to get a good education and to be 'clean' spiritually and morally. Clifford enjoyed going to Heritage House when we were home in Philadelphia. He would help kids, like Lee Morgan, with their music and jam with them."[10]

It was partly his moral example, then, that was missed; but also, Clifford was far and away the best trumpeter of his generation. Taking Fats Navarro's style as his point of departure, he breathed new life into bebop, making it sound as fresh as if it had just been invented. Like Navarro, Brown had a fat, "buttery" sound and played long melodic lines that lent his solos a sense of effortless, flowing ease. This similarity may derive partly from both men's work with Tadd Dameron. Speaking of both Navarro and Brown, Dameron commented: "I used to tell him, 'Fats, when you play a solo, you're going from your first eight bars into your second eight, that's where you really play—those turnbacks.' That helped him a lot. I used to tell him, 'Look, there's where you can tell whether a man can really blow—when he starts playing that eighth and ninth bar and then when he comes out of the middle into the last eight. Those turnbacks mean so much.' I told Clifford that too. I tell all my soloists that."[11] Negotiating such "turnbacks," including the ones leading into and out of the bridges on thirty-two-bar songs (the "bridge" being the B element in an A-A-B-A pattern) has always been one of jazz's trickier undertakings. Failure to do so elegantly creates an effect of rigidity, of being trapped by the song's structure, similar to that of a soloist hewing too closely to a tune's chords because he's not familiar with them.

Brownie extended Navarro's style. He played with more vibrato, especially on ballads; and at faster tempos he employed half-valve effects, slurs, and grace notes that gave his solos a wryly puckish quality. (These effects were later developed still further by Lee Morgan.) "Ebullient," "effervescent," "elated," and "exultant" were words applied to his improvisational style. His ballads were soaringly romantic rather than somber. "Pent-up House," recorded three months before his death on the LP *Sonny Rollins Plus 4* (with Richie Powell, bassist George Morrow, and Max Roach) is a good example of his solo style. The trumpet statement crackles with fire and swing. Tuneful phrases and shouts of pleasure fill every chorus. Rarely has modern jazz radiated so much sweetness, light, and sheer élan. In the article already quoted, Quincy Jones said: "Here was the perfect amalgamation of natural creative ability, and the proper amount of technical training, enabling him to contribute precious moments of musical and emotional expression. This inventiveness placed him in a class far beyond that of most of his poll-winning contemporaries. Clifford's self-assuredness in his playing reflected the mind and soul of a blossoming young artist who would have rightfully taken his place next to Charlie Parker, Dizzy Gillespie, and Miles Davis and other leaders in jazz."[12] By 1956 Brownie *had* taken his place beside such greats. Although Jones is right to suggest that he might have developed further, he had already "made it," and his influence would be audible through the rest of the decade in young hornmen like Lee Morgan and Donald Byrd.

For the last year and a half of the Brown–Roach ensemble's existence, Sonny Rollins shared the front line with Clifford Brown. We have already met Rollins as one of Jackie McLean's pals and a fellow student at Benjamin Franklin High School in New York City. McLean, in a long interview with A. B. Spellman, recalled the Harlem jazz scene in the late 1940s and Rollins's place in it: "Sonny influenced everybody uptown, playing every instrument. There were a lot of musicians in our neighborhood like [drummer] Art Taylor, [pianist] Kenny Drew, Connie Henry, who played bass for a while, Arthur Phipps, who also played bass, and [alto saxophonist] Ernie Henry, and there were guys who used to come from out of the neighborhood to see what was happening, like Walter Bishop. Sonny was the leader of all of them. And when Miles came to town he began to hang up there on the Hill with us."[13]

By 1949 Rollins was recording with beboppers like Babs Gonzales, Bud Powell, and J.J. Johnson. On these sides, he was still digesting Bird's structural precepts and phraseology, but his playing already had fluidity, coherence, and a lithe, off-center rhythmic sense that show why he was held in such esteem by older musicians.

After gigging around New York with Powell, Tadd Dameron, and Art Blakey, Rollins set out for Chicago, where he spent some time in drummer Ike Day's band. In 1951 he was back in New York, appearing live with Miles Davis and participating in Davis's *Dig* session with McLean et al. On the title cut, Rollins stretches out for the first time on record, and you can hear how he has developed. His tone is smooth and lustrous, his phrasing legato, and he shows a flair for songlike melodic figures interspersed with standard bebop licks. At the time, Rollins was still in thrall to Bird, but on "In a Sentimental Mood," recorded two years later with the Modern Jazz Quartet, he also pays homage to Coleman Hawkins, his first idol. Here, in a husky, swaggering treatment of the theme, Sonny reveals a more sanguine tone, complete with growls and hints of Ben Webster–like breathiness. An even clearer example of Hawkins's enduring presence is "Silk 'n' Satin," another ballad and Sonny's first recorded masterpiece. Rollins offers a heartfelt interpretation of his own tune, delivered with all the impassioned authority of a Swing titan. His solo is based on the melody rather than just the chords, while Elmo Hope's stately, almost dirgelike accompaniment intensifies things considerably.

In 1954 Sonny again headed for Chicago. It wasn't until the end of 1955 that he emerged from his self-imposed exile. Bedeviled by drug problems, Rollins had shown up for his first record session as a leader in 1951 "disheveled" (in Joe Goldberg's words) and with "his horn held around his neck by a rope."[14] Now, however, he was "clean" and replaced saxophonist Harold Land in the Roach-Brown ensemble. Though he had always been considered a promising musician, the quantum leap in the power and originality of his playing was astonishing. On "There's No Business Like Show Business" (from *Worktime,* December 1955, his first date as a leader after his "return"), he shows a marked increase in authority, twisting the tune out of shape, reinventing it with surprising hesitations and rhythmic displacements, slowing things down to half time, returning to the theme, punctuating angular runs with gutsy cries delivered in a searing tone, fragmenting and reassembling his materials in the course of eccentrically accented up-tempo flights, and topping it all off with a throaty cadenza. This is our first look at Rollins as a tenor giant with a loose, double-jointed sense of rhythm, unexpectedly patterned phrases, deep swing, and a dark, husky delivery alternating with smoother, Bird-like intonations.

On this record and others (including the *Sonny Rollins Plus 4* date with Clifford Brown and *Saxophone Colossus,* featuring pianist Tommy Flanagan, bassist Doug Watkins, and Max Roach), Rollins established a reputation as the most original and compelling saxophonist since Charlie Parker. The full-bodied emotionality of his style, and his raw, expressive sound, also led him to be universally associated with the emerging hard-bop school centered in New York City. And his gift for thematic improvisations, somewhat unusual in modern jazz, attracted the attention of critics like Gunther Schuller, who wrote a widely noted essay on Rollins. Schuller's piece, "Sonny Rollins and the Challenge of Thematic Improvisation" (originally published in *Jazz Review*) is an incisive attempt to demonstrate through a close analysis of "Blue Seven," a slow, walking blues on *Saxophone Colossus,* that "with Rollins thematic and structural unity have at last achieved the importance in *pure* improvisation that elements such as swing, melodic conception and originality of expression have already enjoyed for years."[15]

In a way less likely to attract the attention of highbrows like
Schuller, Horace Silver (whose last name, a corruption of
"Silva," reflects his Cape Verdean ancestry) was also playing
solos based on carefully structured elaboration of melodic
motifs in the early 1950s. In the liner notes for his LP *Serenade
to a Soul Sister* (Blue Note), Silver listed his "guide lines to
musical composition":

A. Melodic Beauty
B. Meaningful Simplicity
C. Harmonic Beauty
D. Rhythm
E. Environmental, Hereditary, Regional, and Spiritual
   Influences

Of these, "meaningful simplicity" is by far the most significant. Horace's improvisational style has always relied on the
creative use of space and on an inexhaustible supply of striking, songlike figures. His compositions, usually for five pieces
(the "classic" bebop lineup of trumpet, sax, piano, bass, and
drums) and often voiced in 4ths and 5ths to give ensembles a
"fuller" sound, are crystallizations of his solo style, which
abounds in blues-and-gospel-based figures. As part of his apprenticeship, Silver memorized Avery Parrish's piano solo on
Erskine Hawkins's recording of "After Hours." Phrases lifted
from Parrish's solo and from the standard blues and boogie-
woogie repertoire of "funky licks" crop up on many tunes that
are not actually blues—an element of Silver's playing that had
a huge impact on other pianists in the late fifties. Incorporating
material from jazz's "roots" into his music, he passed on many
of his own favorite phrases, which today remain embedded in
the jazz vocabulary.

Born in 1928 in Norwalk, Connecticut, Silver studied piano
in high school with a church organist. While performing in
Hartford with Harold Holdt in 1950, he was heard by Stan
Getz, who hired him to play in his quintet. Horace remained
with Getz into 1951, when he settled in New York City,

gigging as a sideman with Art Blakey, Coleman Hawkins, Oscar Pettiford, Lester Young, and others. By 1954, he was one of the most sought-after pianists in jazz. In the latter part of that year, Silver led a quartet at Minton's that included tenor saxophonist Hank Mobley and Doug Watkins. Asked by Blue Note Records to assemble a quintet for a recording date, Horace called upon Mobley, Watkins, Kenny Dorham, and Art Blakey. The ensemble took the name "Jazz Messengers," which had been used by Blakey in the late forties both for a seventeen-piece band he had led around New York and for a septet that had recorded for Blue Note. Thus, one of hard bop's most influential combos was born.

This cooperative unit, which was to stay together with its original personnel for nearly two years, emphasized swing, emotional openness, and receptivity to older black musical traditions. Along with Silver, the key ingredient in the band was Art Blakey, who at thirty-six was already something of a veteran. Blakey's first spurt of development had occurred during a three-year stint with the Billy Eckstine band. By the time the band broke up in 1947, he was acknowledged by both fellow musicians and aficionados as one of the best young drummers around. He had already shown what he could do on recorded small-group sessions—for example with Fats Navarro or Thelonious Monk—as well as with his own group, the original Jazz Messengers.

In 1947 Blakey went to West Africa, where he remained for two years. Although he denies that this experience influenced his drumming, common sense would indicate the opposite. In any case, what is certain is that when he returned, he played with considerably more maturity and was soon among the most highly regarded musicians in New York City. A list of his employers during the early fifties will indicate the esteem he enjoyed: Clifford Brown, Miles Davis, Charlie Parker, Sonny Stitt, and a host of others, including Buddy De Franco, with whom he spent a year before getting together with Silver to form the second, cooperative Jazz Messengers in 1955.

By that time, Blakey had developed a fiercely individual style that was simultaneously volcanic and severe. Blakey was among the least superfluously "busy" drummers in jazz. His rhythmic sense was so sharp, and his foot and wrist control so precise, that he needed do little more than "keep time" to create an atmosphere of tremendous power. His accompanying figures, sparingly used, came at the right moments to support the soloist with sudden bursts of energy. Likewise, Blakey's solos were usually structured around a few melodic motifs played against each other contrapuntally as he built to a climax. Musical coherence was never sacrificed to technical flash.

The cut on this first collective outing, entitled *Horace Silver and the Jazz Messengers*, that made the deepest impression on musicians was Silver's gospel-flavored "The Preacher." The composition grew out of his habit of playing "Show Me the Way to Go Home" as his final number of the evening. "The Preacher," however, nearly went unrecorded, since Alfred Lion of Blue Note, in Horace's words, "said it was too old-timey, that no one would go for it."[16] The tune was indeed old-timey, "corny" in bebop terms, showing that, again in Silver's words, the Jazz Messengers could "reach way back and get that old time, gutbucket barroom feeling with just a taste of the back-beat."[17] Fired by the song's rocking beat, Dorham and Mobley soar into blues-drenched, vocally inflected solos. Silver follows with a typically stripped-down statement, built around first a two-chord percussive figure and then a descending run, each repeated. Before taking the tune out, the band riffs behind his funky noodling in classic call-and-response fashion.

"Doodlin'," a medium-tempo blues with a two-beat feel, is another of Horace's excursions into the black popular tradition. His solo is phrased in the timeless language of the blues, with barely a nod to bebop's vocabulary. As in "The Preacher," his playing is motif-based and sparely percussive. These motifs then turn into insistent riffs behind Mobley and Dorham.

Dorham in particular enters into the spirit of things, using a lexicon that antedates modern jazz. The soloist who most closely parallels Silver, however, is Blakey, whose improvisation is as starkly melodic as the pianist's is percussive.

Listened to more than thirty years later, tunes like "Doodlin'" and "The Preacher" no longer sound as earth-shattering as they did in 1955. After all, Charlie Parker and other beboppers had composed simple, earthy blues too. One of Bird's tunes, "Now's the Time," was used as the basis for an R & B hit called "The Hucklebuck." Nonetheless, the Jazz Messengers hit at a time when young black musicians were eager to embrace an amalgam of bebop and popular tradition. Likewise, Afro-Cuban influences had been frequent in bebop (for example, Dizzy Gillespie's "Manteca" and Tadd Dameron's "Casbah"). In fact, such Caribbean elements go back at least as far as New Orleans pianist and composer Jelly Roll Morton, one of whose most intriguing maxims, transcribed by Alan Lomax, was "If you can't manage to put tinges of Spanish in your tunes, you will never be able to get the right seasoning, I call it, for jazz."[18] "Spanish tinges," also known as "Latin," "Afro-Cuban," and "Eastern" in black music, are frequent in Silver's and Blakey's work together, cropping up in performances like "Ecaroh" and "Nica's Dream." In hard bop, such tunes, usually featuring sinuously minor melodies and strong rhythmic patterning, were to be part of every working band's repertoire.

Heavier use of the minor mode and strong rhythmic patterning, along with slower tempos, blues- and gospel-influenced phrasing and compositions, and sometimes lusher melodies were all characteristic of hard bop as it emerged in the mid-fifties. In addition, the new music was an opening out in many directions, an unfolding of much that had been implicit in bebop but held in check by its formulas. While musicians like Brown, Silver, and Blakey were all accused of playing "simplified" versions of bebop, each of them found a personal voice by fusing what had been done in the late forties with more popular elements. As a result, jazz regained a measure of

acceptance in black neighborhoods and reaffirmed its connections with terpsichorean rhythms. As Art Blakey said in a 1956
interview in *Down Beat:* "When we're on the stand, and we see
that there are people in the audience who aren't patting their
feet and who aren't nodding their heads to our music, we know
we're doing something wrong. Because when we do get our
message across, those heads and feet do move."[19]

B

A NEW MAINSTREAM

Branching Out

In the 1950s, the critic Stanley Dance coined the term "Main-stream" for jazz of the Depression years (approximately 1930–1940). In Dance's words: "Primarily, it is a reference term for a vast body of jazz that was at one time in some danger of losing its identity. Practically, it is applied to the jazz idiom which developed between the heyday of King Oliver and Jelly Roll Morton on the one hand and that of Charlie Parker and Dizzy Gillespie on the other.

"The tag originated during the recent period when jazz seemed to be entirely divided between Traditional (alias Dixie-land, alias New Orleans, alias Two-Beat) and modern (alias Bop, alias Cool, alias Progressive). Among those this division left out in the cold were musicians like Duke Ellington, Earl Hines, Count Basie, Coleman Hawkins and Buck Clayton. Since all good jazz, of whatever kind and era, theoretically swings, 'Swing' was hardly an adequate label for them. Hence 'Mainstream' for jazz of a 'central' kind, a music not inhibited by any particular instrumental combination, but emphasizing the twin virtues of communicable emotional expression and swing."[1]

As we have seen, stress on these "twin virtues" was also

typical of hard bop, which resembles Dance's concept of Mainstream in other ways as well. For one thing, it too is "in danger
of losing its identity" as it is collapsed into bebop by current
terminology. As with Dance's Mainstream, hard bop was
wedged in between two styles (bebop and the "free jazz" of
altoist Ornette Coleman, pianist Cecil Taylor, and others) that
were easier to define in a few sentences. As bebop turned into
something broader and more flexible in the mid-fifties, and as a
style known simply as "modern jazz"—meaning it lacked
bebop's readily identifiable characteristics but had absorbed
its advances—took shape, people began talking about "mainstream modernism." Jazz has always been a volatile music,
changing quickly and often, and the hard-bop period (like the
heyday of Swing or Mainstream) represents a moment of
balance and polish in the work of many musicians, with more
emphasis on perfecting an existing style than on self-
consciously breaking new ground.

Yet neither period was one of stagnation. For one thing, the
elegant equilibriums thus achieved cannot be sustained for
long. Such styles generate their own pressures for radical
change. In addition, the leaders of both Dance's Mainstream
and the modern-jazz one were eclectic in their approaches and
therefore open to change—but by accretion rather than rup-
ture. Duke Ellington, for example, went on evolving, absorbing new elements and elaborating old ones, until the end of his
life. Some of his finest work—records like *And His Mother
Called Him Bill, New Orleans Suite, The Far East Suite,* and
Afro-Bossa—dates from the 1960s, and (in the case of *New
Orleans Suite*) 1970. The fact that Mainstream jazz didn't "all
sound alike" (in the sense that to some degree bebop or New
Orleans jazz did) gave him room to expand and unfold while
retaining a sense of continuity. In this he was paralleled by the
openness of musicians like Rollins and Coltrane to the beginnings of free jazz, as well as to developments within hard bop
like the advent of modally based improvisation.

Thus the hard-bop period, like the Mainstream one, was a

time of both consolidation *and* expansion. Yet the exact nature of the shifts in perspective that brought jazz into a more diverse and expressive realm in the 1950s has eluded many jazz writers, who have been satisfied with clichés about soul, funk, and "returning to the roots." Though the decade was a time of renewed interest among jazz musicians in blues and gospel, these were only two tinctures among many in a broadened musical palette that ranged from classical impressionism to the dirtiest gutbucket effects. By 1955, bebop was treated by jazzmen as but one genre among many. Hard bop functioned as an opening out in numerous directions.

What this opening out meant will be clearer if we look, for example, at the pianists who emerged in the late fifties, offering a gamut of approaches that reworked, altered, and at times subverted the bebop idiom. Among these were Tommy Flanagan, Kenny Drew, Herbie Nichols, Mal Waldron, Horace Silver, Randy Weston, Ray Bryant, Sonny Clark, Elmo Hope, and Wynton Kelly. What a variety of emotional and stylistic orientations these names conjure up! Though all were of approximately the same generation and took bebop as their point of departure, their styles ranged from Ray Bryant's light-fingered, Teddy Wilson–tinted musings to the starkly minimalist, fiercely driving solos of Mal Waldron, with infinite tones between and around them. As an alternate approach, one might take a single pianist like Kenny Drew and find in his playing many of the period's dominant tendencies: "funk" (extensive use of blues voicings on tunes that are not strictly blues), Debussyesque lyrical embellishments, finger-busting up-tempo solos, and multiple references to earlier styles both gently contemplative (Teddy Wilson and Nat Cole) and hot and bluesy (stride piano via Monk). In such an eclectic context, it's not surprising that many more pianists with individually recognizable styles appeared in the fifties than in the forties. Though hard bop was certainly a return to the pulsing rhythms and earthy emotions of jazz's "roots," it was much else besides.

This "much else" has always made a precise definition of hard bop difficult. Like many labels attached to artistic movements (for example, "symbolism" in poetry or "abstract expressionism" in painting), "hard bop" is a vague one; and the fact that it refers above all to an expansive movement both formally and emotionally makes it still more elusive. Nonetheless, one might tentatively break the school down into four groups.

1. Musicians on the borderline between jazz and the popular black tradition: for instance, Horace Silver, alto saxophonist Cannonball Adderley, and organist Jimmy Smith. Artists like these, whose LPs and singles often appeared on *Billboard*'s charts, drew heavily on urban blues (Jimmy Smith's "Midnight Special"), gospel (Horace Silver's "The Preacher"), and Latin American music (Cannonball Adderley's "Jive Samba"). Without renouncing bebop's discoveries, their heavy beat and blues-influenced phrasing won broad popular appeal, reestablishing jazz as a staple on ghetto jukeboxes.

2. More astringent, less popular musicians, whose work is starker and more tormented: for instance, saxophonists Jackie McLean and Tina Brooks and pianists Mal Waldron and Elmo Hope. Such musicians, some of whom (Brooks and Hope among them) never achieved recognition outside a small circle of jazzmen and aficionados, also played music that was more expressive emotionally but less stunning technically than bebop had been. The mood of their work, however, tended to be somber. They favored the minor mode, and their playing possessed a sinister—sometimes tragic—air not unlike the atmosphere of, say, Billie Holiday's "You're My Thrill."

3. Musicians of a gentler, more lyrical bent who found in hard bop a more congenial climate than bebop had offered: for instance, trumpeter Art Farmer, composers Benny Golson and Gigi Gryce, and pianists Hank Jones and Tommy Flanagan. In a sense, such musicians were not hard boppers at all. They are, however, partially associated with the movement for two

reasons. First, they often performed and recorded with hard boppers. Art Farmer, for example, played in Horace Silver's quintet and with saxophonists Jackie McLean and Jimmy Heath. And second, the very latitude and diversity of hard bop allowed room for their more meditative styles to evolve. Hard bop's slower tempos and simpler melodies also helped, as did the school's overall aesthetic, which favored "saying something" over technical bravado.

4. Experimentalists consciously trying to expand jazz's structural and technical boundaries: for instance, pianist Andrew Hill, Sonny Rollins, and John Coltrane prior to his 1965 record *Ascension.* This category would also include Thelonious Monk and Charles Mingus, whose playing and compositions were at once experimental and reminiscent of the moods and forms of earlier black music, including jazz of the 1920s and 1930s. Mingus, for example, composed and recorded "My Jelly Roll Soul," which is simultaneously a tribute to Jelly Roll Morton and a successful attempt to transmute and reformulate Morton's compositional style in modern jazz terms. Monk's solos were notable for their mixture of dissonance and such pre-bebop modes as stride piano, often playfully juxtaposed. These musicians, by influencing and challenging those in categories 1 and 2, kept hard bop from stagnation. Even at their most volcanic, their performances were pervaded by a sense of thoughtful searching.

Thus, a mainstream is actually a complicated set of interlocking worlds and tendencies. Indeed, many hard boppers could easily adapt their styles to the requirements of the occasion. Even Horace Silver, more identified than any other single musician with hard bop's "down-home" variant, composed some of modern jazz's most poignant ballads: tunes like "Shirl," "Lonely Woman," "Peace," "Sweet Stuff," and "Cherry Blossom." In addition, Silver was something of an innovator in his compositions, venturing into time signatures (like the $\frac{6}{8}$ he used on one of his first major hits, "Señor

Blues") and bar lengths (like the 16-6-16-bar structure of "Swinging the Samba") that broke with jazz's traditional Tin Pan Alley–derived thirty-two-bar A-A-B-A formula.

Though most of Silver's recordings exemplify hard-bop-as-modern-mainstream, perhaps the most successful crystallization of his style as pianist, composer, and bandleader in the late 1950s was *Further Explorations.* This LP featured Art Farmer, tenor saxophonist Clifford Jordan, bassist Teddy Kotick, and drummer Louis Hayes. At the time it was recorded, the quintet had been playing together for many months and had evolved into one of the best-integrated combos in jazz. Its repertoire consisted almost entirely of Silver's tunes (only one of the six cuts on *Further Explorations,* Harold Arlen's "Ill Wind," is a standard). These were by no means casual heads for blowing but rather genuine jazz compositions. Several are unusual in their construction (for example, "Melancholy Mood," with its 7-7-7-bar pattern), and most include secondary themes, varied rhythmic devices (typically consisting of a Latin beat played off against straight-ahead $\frac{4}{4}$ sections), and percussive riffs.

None of the tunes is blues- or gospel-based, and only one is truly up-tempo: the shortest cut on the LP, "Safari," an early Silver composition first recorded in a trio version with bassist Gene Ramey and Art Blakey in 1952. Each is "original" in its chord structure—that is, not based on earlier pop songs. All these factors help create an atmosphere of careful craftsmanship, as well as providing springboards much like those used by big bands in the 1930s to recharge and propel soloists.

Among the sidemen, Farmer most nearly equals Silver in brilliance and maturity. Farmer's sound is simultaneously burnished and slightly tart, while his solos are elegantly constructed. Usually his lines stay in the middle register, and he saves strategically placed outbursts in the upper reaches of his horn for moments of particular intensity. Jordan's style is somewhat less thoughtful, and Sonny Rollins's influence on him is obvious. Just as obvious, however, is his place within a nucleus of hard-blowing Chicago saxophonists of the fifties that included Johnny Griffin, John Gilmore, Charles Davis, and John Jenkins. Jordan's robustly bluesy phrasing, his honks and soulful wails, and his warm, slightly breathy sound all create an effective contrast to Farmer's more restrained and delicate approach.

But the star of the record is Silver. His crisp articulation and his melodic imagination, his combination of fierce precision and relaxed swing all contribute to an unmistakable musical fingerprint. On "Melancholy Mood," a ballad and the one trio cut, he creates a particularly striking solo. Silver's ballad style is one of his most exquisite achievements and a good example of what he meant by "meaningful simplicity." His phrases, always ringingly percussive, are here transmuted by the tune's singing romanticism. Octave tremolos, transposed and repeated phrases, the careful deployment of funky licks that anchor the piece in the black tradition—all are elements of this beautifully realized solo.

Most tracks on *Further Explorations* incorporate Latin rhythms, and this pervasive aspect of Silver's work must derive partly from his family background. His father was an immigrant from the Cape Verdean Islands, and the pianist's recollections of his childhood evoke his family's way of life and his father's music: "He loved to play music: he plays guitar, a little violin, all by ear and all Cape Verdean–Portuguese folk music, mostly in the minor key, very simple, not too many chord changes . . . When I was a kid my father and my uncles used to give house parties a lot of times. The women—my mother and some of my uncles' girlfriends—they would all prepare food. Somebody would bring a bottle of whisky, someone wine. The party would be in the kitchen— we had a large kitchen—and the place would be packed with people dancing. My father and uncles would play the music on the guitar, the violin and the mandolin. It's different from the authentic Portuguese music from Portugal—but I suppose it's derivative of that. I remember as a kid when they would have some of those parties I would have on those pajamas that your feet go into, that cover you all up. I'd go to sleep, but then they'd be laughing and talking and dancing and I'd wake up in the middle of the night. I'd hear the music and I'd get out of bed and go down the steps and sit on the edge of the steps and peek around and listen to the music and watch them dance. Somebody would bring me over something to eat, some potato salad or chicken or something, and let me stay a while."[2]

Later, in the 1960s, Silver recorded "Song for My Father" (*Cantiga para meu pai*), his most commercially successful tune, covered by James Brown among others. In the same interview cited above, Silver described the composition's genesis: "My dad through the years had always said to me, 'Why don't you take some of this Portuguese folk music and put it into jazz?' I never could see it. To me it always seemed corny— because I was born here into American music, whether it be jazz or whatever. But there is a feeling there: there's something there that's valid. I didn't really get in tune with that feeling until I was invited by Sergio Mendes to his house in Rio de Janeiro. I went to see Carnival and went around to different places he was playing and sat in, and I was fascinated by the musical capabilities of some of the young musicians down there. They were all into this bossa nova thing, which as you know was greatly inspired by our American jazz. I got turned onto that beat. So I got back to New York and I said, 'I'll try to write a tune using that rhythm.' I started fooling around and I came up with the melody and I realized the melody I came up with was akin to Cape Verdean—like something my dad would play. That was 'Song for My Father.'"

If Silver's rhythmically charged playing and fondness for the minor mode derive from his Afro-Iberian heritage, his affinity with the blues reflects his interests during the years when he was discovering North America's indigenous music: "My first introduction to jazz was boogie-woogie. Back in the days when boogie was prevalent, when Tommy Dorsey had a tune called

'Boogie-Woogie'—it was Pinetop Smith's tune. Dorsey had an arrangement of that which I copied off the records and played by ear. Then Earl Fatha Hines had a 'Boogie-Woogie on the St. Louis Blues'—I copied that off the record by ear. Eddie Heywood had a boogie-woogie arrangement on 'Begin the Beguine'—I copied that off the record by ear. I copied some of Jay McShann off the records. I was about 12. I used to be the hit at the little teenage parties."

Silver also listened to the blues: "I liked and still do like all them old downhome blues singers like Muddy Waters, Lightning Hopkins, Peetie Wheatstraw (the devil's son-in-law), Memphis Minnie. I dig the feeling. They weren't technicians but they had a whole lot of feeling. It was diamonds in the rough, unpolished diamonds."

A feeling for the blues' stark economy and a search for "meaningful simplicity" were also characteristic of Miles Davis, who in the late fifties led another "classic" and very popular modern-mainstream quintet featuring John Coltrane, pianist Red Garland, bassist Paul Chambers, and Philly Joe Jones. In an interview with Amiri Baraka, Davis said of this band and the one that followed it: "I used to tell them, 'The bass got the tonic. Don't play in the same register as the sax. Lay out. Don't play . . . I always listen to what I can leave out."[3]

The Davis group, which remained together as a unit from late 1955 until the spring of 1957, is often considered the most influential combo of its time. Any one of its last five records (*Cookin'*, *Relaxin'*, *Workin'*, and *Steamin'* on Prestige and *'Round About Midnight* on Columbia) could stand as an example of its work. Indeed, the four on Prestige were all recorded on two days in 1956, each number being done in a single take, and then released gradually over a period of several years. The first to hit the stores was *Cookin'*, which featured a Davis original ("Blues by Five"), singer and saxophonist Eddie "Cleanhead" Vinson's "Tune Up," a composition by Sonny

Rollins ("Airegin"), another by Swing altoist Benny Carter ("When Lights Are Low"), and the Richard Rodgers ballad "My Funny Valentine."

The feeling on *Cookin'* is far more spontaneous than on *Further Explorations.* There are no secondary themes, and the whole formal framework suggests a "blowing session" rather than the kind of careful preparation evident on the Silver LP. Yet if a "blowing session" implies musicians unfamiliar with one another's work, then *Cookin'* is anything but! For one thing, Garland, Chambers, and Jones comprised one of the most cohesive rhythm sections in the history of jazz, a trio closely attuned to each other and to Davis and Coltrane. In addition, as Joe Goldberg observed: "At least part of the unique quality of the quintet performances lay in a particular principle which Davis grasped, a principle so simple that it apparently eluded everyone else. To put it in terms of this particular group, a quintet is not always a quintet. It could also be a quartet featuring Miles, and, at different times on the same tune, it could be a quartet featuring Coltrane or a trio featuring either Garland or Chambers. The Davis rhythm section, Jones in particular, was well aware of this, and gave each of the three principal soloists his own best backing. Behind Davis, the rhythm was full of space, with few chords; behind Coltrane, it was compulsive; and with Garland, it lapsed into an easy, [Ahmad] Jamal like feeling."[4] Finally, a few timbral devices— Garland's use of block chords in the style of Ahmad Jamal or Erroll Garner, Chambers's bowed solos, and Davis's mute-in-microphone approach to ballads—added textural variety.

Davis's ballads enabled him to reach an audience far broader than jazz aficionados and made him in a sense the greatest jazz torch singer since Billie Holiday. Playing the microphone as much as his horn, he produced a sound, quivery and haunting, charged with restrained passion, that dominates "My Funny Valentine." Unmuted on the other tunes, he also makes the most of his sound, which seems to contain depths and nuances lacking in other trumpeters. At times jauntily ironic, at times playing in a hoarsely anguished whisper, Davis creates a set of solos in which silence, used for dramatic impact, punctuates striking figures from which all extraneous embellishments have been burned away. This is particularly true on the medium-tempo "Blues by Five," but even on up-tempo numbers Davis refuses to be hurried and sometimes slows his own tempo to half that of the rest of the quintet.

Coltrane, who to some critics seemed to sort so ill with Davis, was in fact the trumpeter's ideal foil. Over a more volcanic Philly Joe, he unleashes a firestorm of convoluted phrases that alternate with simpler gutbucket figures (Coltrane had paid extensive "dues" in R & B bands, including Daisy May and the Hep Cats and King Kolax's combo), piercing cries, and melodic fragments tumbling over each other as though he hadn't time to say everything he wanted to. As fiery as Davis is severe, Coltrane strains against bar lines and chord changes. The contrast between the two is crucial to the group's impact. Nearly as important, however, are Chambers's dark, woody sound and choice notes and Philly Joe's volatile, double-jointed rhythmic sense. Speaking of the drummer, whose life was even more disordered than usual for a jazz musician of the era, Davis told Nat Hentoff: "Look, I wouldn't care if he came up on the bandstand in his B.V.D.s and with one arm, just so long as he was there. He's got the fire I want. There's nothing more terrible than playing with a dull rhythm section. Jazz has got to have *that thing.* You have to be born with it. You can't even buy it. If you could buy it, they'd have it at the next Newport festival."[5]

Davis's and Silver's quintets were perhaps the two most influential hard-bop bands of the late fifties. Funky yet sophisticated, formally innovative without straining to draw attention to themselves on this count (certainly no one would confuse them with any *earlier* style of jazz), they both embodied and created the hip sound of urban America. Mainstream hard bop, however, consisted of far more than its "stars" and by 1958 was the common currency of virtually all gifted black musicians. Among these were pianists Wynton Kelly, Elmo Hope, and Sonny Clark. None was enormously successful in a commercial sense, but their lives and music embody hard bop's underside: a penumbral world where most of the era's best jazzmen suffered and created.

Scufflin': Three Pianists

Born in Jamaica, Wynton Kelly (1931–1971) came to the United States at the age of four and grew up in Brooklyn. He made his professional debut in 1943, and two years later he toured the Caribbean with Ray Abrams's combo. Gigs with bands somewhere between jazz and R & B followed, and in the early fifties Kelly also worked and recorded with such giants as Lester Young, Dizzy Gillespie, and J.J. Johnson. His first LP as a leader, never reissued, was a ten-inch trio date for Blue Note. In the mid-fifties, he spent three years as Dinah Washington's accompanist, and it was during this period that he began to establish himself as an unusually engaging, light-fingered stylist as well as (in record producer Orrin Keepnews's words) "possibly the finest jazz accompanist of our day."[6]

In the late fifties and early sixties, Kelly seems to have recorded with virtually every major jazz soloist: John Coltrane, Sonny Rollins, guitarist Wes Montgomery, Jimmy Heath, Johnny Griffin, and a host of others, including Miles Davis, with whom he spent the years between 1959 and 1963, replacing Red Garland in Miles's band. In the course of the same period, Kelly recorded several albums as a leader for Riverside and Vee Jay. After leaving Miles in 1963, the pianist formed a trio with two other Davis alumni: Paul Chambers and drummer Jimmy Cobb, cohorts in what was by then widely regarded as jazz's most swinging rhythm section. Wes Montgomery later joined the unit for concert and club appearances, some of which were recorded by Verve Records.

Throughout these years, Kelly's ebullience, phenomenal swing, and deep empathy with the blues (which earned him the invitation to sit in on "Freddie Freeloader" for Davis's *Kind of Blue* album) made him a favorite with other musicians. Yet Kelly seemed unable to escape the typecast role of sideman. Bill Evans's admiring words, quoted in Leonard Feather's and Ira Gitler's *Encyclopedia of Jazz in the 1970s*, express an appreciation that Kelly only rarely won outside an inner circle of his peers: "When I heard him in Dizzy's big band, the whole thing was so joyful and exuberant; nothing about it seemed calculated. And yet, with the clarity of the way he played, you know he had to put this together in a very carefully planned way—but the result was completely without calculation, there was just a pure shining through the conception."[7] Perhaps it was his apparent casualness, as if swinging, joyously expressive music came as naturally as breathing, that kept Kelly from the forefront of most listeners' awareness. A heavy drinker for years, he died in Toronto, apparently of an epileptic seizure.

Full View, an LP recorded for the Milestone label with bassist Ron McClure and Jimmy Cobb, was Wynton Kelly's last record as a leader and offers ample opportunity to savor the many graces of his style. The tempos range from slow to medium-up, thus ensuring more swing than technical fireworks—and swing Kelly does, with all the resources in his varied repertoire. The most potent of these, perhaps, is a penchant for lagging slightly behind the beat, especially toward the end of one of those cascading phrases that were his forte. Such figures spiral unevenly downward, their fall broken by occasional upward flights, gathering power toward the end through the delayed rhythm and resultant tension between piano and drums. Though Kelly's lines frequently alternate with block chords and funky octave tremolos, there is no predictable modulation from single-note lines to chords in the manner of many Garland- and Garner-influenced pianists. Instead, Kelly keeps his music bubbling through fine tunings of time and attack and can make a series of eighth notes jump as few other pianists could have done.

The repertoire on *Full View* also reflects Kelly's closeness to popular music, especially in the torch songs ("Born to Be Blue" and "What a Difference a Day Makes," the latter a tune Kelly frequently played with Dinah Washington) and blues pieces ("Scufflin'" and "Dont'cha Hear Me Callin' to Ya," both with the kind of danceable, forward-leaning beat popularized by such jazz hits as Cannonball Adderley's "Jive Samba" and Lee Morgan's "The Sidewinder"). The ballads show off Kelly's adroit pedal work, his silky, caressing touch, and his ability to swing a slow tune without violating its tempo and atmosphere, while the blues reveal the pianist's sublimely dirty sense of the idiom, as does "I Want a Little Girl," a smoldering, rocking slow grind.

The medium-tempo pop tunes ("I Thought" by Rudy Stevenson, "Autumn Leaves," "On a Clear Day," and Burt Bacharach's "Walk on By"), however, probably show Kelly in his most characteristic groove: alternately soulful and airy, tipping light and bearing down hard. The whole record, like Kelly's playing itself, is an object lesson in how to derive maximum rhythmic impetus from an instrument whose tonality is more fixed than any other commonly used in black music. If jazz piano has two sides, an artistically self-conscious one (Art Tatum, Bud Powell, Andrew Hill, et al.) and a "lighter" one closer to the perspectives of our best popular music (Teddy Wilson and Erroll Garner, for example), then Kelly is one of the three or four giants within the latter tradition. His techniques and discoveries, however, have been appropriated by almost everyone—for example, by the "experimentalist" Muhal Richard Abrams in some of his jazzier moments. For sheer sensuality and expressive charm, Kelly is just about unbeatable, and although in his wake scores of musicians have adopted his methods, Kelly himself still haunts those semi-anonymous catacombs inhabited by the shades of "musicians' musicians."

Elmo Hope (1923–1967), who was christened St. Elmo Sylvester Hope after the patron saint of sailors, grew up in Harlem, where he and Bud Powell were close friends. The two young pianists often practiced together and played for each other—both classical music and jazz—and Bud introduced Elmo to his friend Thelonious Monk. Bud, of course, went on to become the most widely imitated pianist of the era, while Elmo remained in the shadows, working mostly with R & B bands, in particular a long (1948–1951) stint with trumpeter Joe Morris. Not until the fifties did Elmo start recording in a jazz context with Sonny Rollins, Lou Donaldson, Clifford Brown, and Jackie McLean. In addition, he cut two ten-inch LPs for Blue Note, a trio set for Prestige, and another featuring John Coltrane and Hank Mobley for the same label.

None of these achievements, however, won Hope much acclaim, and he was usually thought of—by those who knew of his existence—as simply another competent Bud Powell disciple. The problems Hope faced as a heroin addict may also have limited the amount of attention he could devote to his music during this period. All the same, on a tune like "De-Dah," a Hope original from a Clifford Brown–Lou Donaldson album on Blue Note, one can already hear many elements of the pianist's emerging style: somber, internally shifting chords in the introduction; punchy, twisting phrases in his solo; and the smoldering intensity that always characterized his best work.

In 1957, after a spell on the road with trumpeter Chet Baker, Hope decided to settle in Los Angeles. The move, however, proved to be a mistake; and by 1961, in a *Down Beat* interview with John Tynan entitled "Bitter Hope," Elmo advised young West Coast pianists: "This is no place to try to learn anything. If they want to learn, let them go back to New York—both for inspiration and brotherly love. They'll find more things happening."[8] Yet the years in California marked a turning point in Elmo's development. Though generally isolated and denied much chance to record, he made giant strides musically and capped his period in L.A. with two monumental albums for Hifijazz that ensured his place in history. The sides are his own *Elmo Hope Trio* and Harold Land's *The Fox*, on which four of the six tunes are Elmo's. *The Fox* is dominated by his spirit and conception, despite superb performances by the leader, trumpeter Dupree Bolton, bassist Herbie Lewis, and drummer Frank Butler. It was when these albums appeared that jazz critics began to take more notice of Hope. The trio date received five stars, *Down Beat*'s highest rating, and John Tynan's review defined "the essence of Hope" as "a sort of bitter-sweet melancholy that seems to lie at the core of other jazzmen—and other individuals of comparable sensitivity— who sometimes find the world 'a bit much,' as the English say, to cope with."⁹

Not long after the interview, and with the encouragement of Riverside Records' Orrin Keepnews, Elmo decided to take his own advice and return to New York. There he recorded (in June 1961) another major album called *Homecoming* with trumpeter Blue Mitchell, Jimmy Heath, tenor saxophonist Frank Foster, Percy Heath, and Philly Joe Jones. More records followed, including a duet session with his wife Bertha and several trio sets, but gigs were hard to come by despite some work with Johnny Griffin. Poor health and drug problems also plagued the pianist in his last years. Another disc, *Sounds from Riker's Island*, featured a group entirely composed of junkies and an essay by Nat Hentoff attacking America's penal approach to narcotics addiction. On May 19, 1967, Hope died of pneumonia.

Elmo Hope's reputation as a gifted and tragic figure is based, above all, on his trio date for Hifijazz, now available on Contemporary Records. The LP, on which Elmo is backed by one of California's fiercest bass and drum duos (Jimmy Bond and Frank Butler), is evenly divided between dark-toned ballads ("Barfly," "Eejah," "Like Someone in Love," and "Tranquility") and jagged medium-up tunes ("B's a Plenty," "Boa," "Something for Kenny," and "Minor Bertha"). Mostly in the minor mode, Elmo's compositions are dominated by a sense of urgent musical questing as well as by a feeling of self-exposure far beyond standard jazz postures.

Intentionally or not, Hope's solos do everything possible to convey these tonalities and to give the impression that nothing is being played merely as a lick or to fill up space. Ideas and fragments of ideas abruptly spill over and intersect each other, as if the pianist's hands could barely keep pace with his emotions. Bars densely packed with runs and baroque filigrees alternate with stark, dissonant figures or Monkish seconds, wide intervalic leaps, and octaves. Even more than in most modern jazz, melodic units rarely coincide with bar lines, and the sequence of phrases is extremely irregular. Likewise, conventional ballads (such as "Like Someone in Love") are also undercut and transformed by unexpected, violent accents.

All these elements, taken together, create an effect of conventional forms being pushed to their limits under the pressure of Hope's turbulent sensibility. This effect bears a certain resemblance to Andrew Hill's angry, intellectually exploratory work in the mid-sixties, but in Elmo's case molds seem mutilated and broken in a sort of intimate agony. The ballads, of course, with their solemn dignity and nobly "classical" references, convey this sensation especially. Another possible comparison would be with Bud Powell in his later years—that is, if Powell's assault on symmetry and flow had produced not incoherent gestures but some musical correlative for life on the brink.

Hope's harmonic imagination is one of the record's strong points. His voicings are a constant source of surprise, while the chord patterns—especially in ballads like "Barfly"—are fresh and richly textured. Though one can feel the remembered presence of his early musical companions, Elmo possesses his materials absolutely. Indeed, when this record first appeared, some listeners felt that a third great bebop pianist had emerged, after a strangely prolonged incubation, at the very instant when Monk and Powell had lost some of their creative fire. Elmo Hope, at that moment, seemed destined to assume a place among the very finest pianists in jazz history, but he had little chance to build on his achievements. Instead, he left only a few glimpses with which we may conjure what a full and secure career might have offered.

Conrad Yeatis "Sonny" Clark (1931–1963) was born in Herminie, Pennsylvania, a coal-mining town of some eight hundred inhabitants. At the age of twelve, the pianist moved to Pittsburgh and began playing professionally while he was still attending high school. In 1951, he journeyed to the West Coast with an older brother. After deciding to stay, Sonny began gigging around San Francisco with saxophonists Wardell Gray and Vido Musso, Oscar Pettiford, and Buddy De Franco, with whom he stayed from late 1953 till the beginning of 1956. Sonny's next move was down to Los Angeles, where he joined Howard Rumsey's All Stars at the Lighthouse in Hermosa Beach. Asked by Leonard Feather to give his impressions of that experience, Sonny replied: "The climate is crazy. I'm going to be truthful, though: I did have sort of a hard time trying to be comfortable in my playing. The fellows out on the west coast have a different sort of feeling, a different approach to jazz. They swing in their own way. But [drummer] Stan Levey, [trombonist] Frank Rosolino and [trumpeter] Conte Candoli were a very big help; of course they all worked back in the east for a long time during the early part of their careers . . . The eastern musicians play with so much fire and passion."[10]

Like Elmo Hope, Sonny took his own advice and headed for New York, accompanying Dinah Washington along the way "more or less for the ride." Once there, he began to record for Blue Note (four albums: *Dial S for Sonny, Sonny's Crib, Sonny Clark Trio,* and *Cool Struttin'*) and was frequently in clubs and on record sessions with the likes of Stan Getz, Sonny Rollins, Charles Mingus, Clifford Jordan, and Johnny Griffin. The personnel from his own Blue Note sides in the late fifties (including Art Farmer, Donald Byrd, Jackie McLean, John Coltrane, Paul Chambers, Philly Joe Jones, Louis Hayes, and Art Taylor) reads like a *Who's Who* of the New York hard-bop scene in that period.

Although this flurry of activity produced results of varying quality, within a few years Clark had evolved into one of jazz's best pianists. After a brief hiatus in the late fifties, he cut an album (*Max Roach/George Duvivier/Sonny Clark*, later reissued on the Bainbridge label) of such concentrated inventive fire that it could stand comparison with even the quickest-burning bebop torches. During the early sixties, Sonny also recorded with such Blue Note regulars as Jackie McLean and Dexter Gordon, both of whom he matched in fluency and passion. In 1961, the pianist made another album for Blue Note, by far his best on that label and also, as it happened, his last: *Leapin' and Lopin'*.

Less eccentric than Hope but without Kelly's popular, let-the-good-times-roll approach, Sonny Clark never had much trouble finding work. He was one of many musicians encouraged and supported by Blue Note's discerning musical director Alfred Lion; yet, like Kelly and Hope, he was little known outside of jazz's inner coteries. His difficulties in reaching a wider audience were compounded by narcotics addiction, and late in 1962 he was hospitalized after a heart attack. Released in early January 1963, he played his last gig at a New York club called Junior's, where he died of an overdose in the early hours of January 30. To avoid bad publicity and to preserve their liquor license, the owners moved his corpse to a private apartment before calling the police. Bill Evans, who acknowledged his influence and shared both his "problem" and his long-lined, sinuous pianistic approach, dedicated the tune "N.Y.C.'s No Lark" (an anagram of Clark's name) to his late friend.

Though more conventional than Hope's, Sonny Clark's style also seemed to imply great things to come. On the back of his *Cool Struttin'* album (Blue Note), the pianist praises Lennie Tristano's "technical ability and conception," and the debt to Tristano is clear on *Max Roach/George Duvivier/Sonny Clark*. But it is a mixed debt, for Clark's playing seems at first hearing to be so firmly rooted in the Powell tradition that one is hardly prepared to detect Tristano as his second guiding spirit.

The link with Tristano (though also with Powell) is most evident in Sonny Clark's snaking melodic lines. These lines, which can extend for several bars at a time, building through surprisingly accentuated melodic turns, are really the essence of Clark's style and his dominant musical mode. The intensity generated by this onrush of ideas, pouring forth in rapid succession as the long phrases build toward delayed climaxes or, at times, multiple internal ones, lends an air of concentrated taking-care-of-business to the side. Clark's other major influence, however, is Horace Silver, and nearly every cut on this trio set includes at least one bow in the funkmaster's direction—usually in the form of one of his pet phrases. Laced through intricate multi-bar lines but often increasing in frequency as the solo approaches its climax, these phrases turn into another element of surprise within the otherwise unremitting context. They seem to ground Clark's music in the popular tradition, while making few concessions to it and maintaining an atmosphere of charged lucidity quite different from Silver's more relaxed effects.

The record is entirely devoted to Clark originals (mostly medium to medium-up blues or variations on standard chord changes), whose themes tend to be functional. Few chords—other than an occasional third, fourth, or octave—are used in the right hand, and the emphasis is almost exclusively on single-note lines. One exception, however, is "My Conception," an unaccompanied ballad played mostly out of tempo, with the slightest hint of stride in the last chorus. Here Clark's appreciation of Art Tatum's lush virtuosity is expressed in meditative clusters of runs, embellishments, and two-handed, contrapuntal figures.

Rhythmically, on most numbers Clark tends to push the beat for an effect of urgency, rather than retard it for a laid-back groove as Kelly would have done. Clark's staccato attack fits in well with the serpentine structurings he favored, and his playing makes one feel that all the bebop and blues vocabulary ever required was musicians who employed it with sufficient conviction. Clark seemed to be such a musician, and many expected great things from him: a career in which the record with Roach and Duvivier would merely be the opening statement, showing he had assimilated his sources and was ready to take off on his own.

This success, of course, never occurred, nor did Kelly and Hope reach the sort of public they deserved. Jazz has always been a minority taste, and few listeners have been able to keep more than a dozen names in their minds simultaneously. Critics, also, have often had an overly schematic approach to the music, devoting attention to those they deem major innovators at the expense of equally talented musicians whose individuality is expressed in subtler ways. (The amount of ink expended on Lester Young, as opposed to Ben Webster, is a good example of this phenomenon.) Such an approach has been particularly unfortunate when applied to hard bop and to Dance's Mainstream. Like the style Dance championed, hard bop was "a vast body of music." Part of its richness—and part of the reason so many hard-bop record dates are being reissued today—is the school's extraordinary depth and range of figures. That, of course, was what made it "mainstream": almost everyone good was playing it!

4!

THE SCENE

Jazz in the Ghetto

Critics usually assume that jazz ceased to be "popular music" with the arrival of bebop in the mid-1940s. While this assumption is partly true, it also requires a good deal of qualification. Jazz, like blues, remained economically viable in black neighborhoods until driven out by the pop sounds of the late 1960s. That jazz (with the exception of the "cool" style played by Stan Getz, Gerry Mulligan, and others) had a primarily black audience is confirmed by Joe Fields, currently with Muse Records and formerly employed by Prestige and Columbia: "Our records sold to some white college kids, but our sales [at Prestige] were overwhelmingly to blacks—not just tenor and organ stuff but hard bop too. That's why what we sold in Boston was *nothing* compared to Chicago, St. Louis, Cleveland . . . Our sales in Los Angeles were much better than in San Francisco."

To understand this world is also to understand why, although jazz is currently enjoying one of its periods of greatest popularity among whites, the flow of talented black teenagers into the music has been reduced to a trickle. From 1945 to 1965, jazz attracted the ghetto's most gifted young musicians.

During the late 1950s and early 1960s, hard bop was the basic idiom in the neighborhoods where such youngsters lived. Less intellectual and less technically dazzling than bebop before it, hard bop was also more open to the black popular tradition—especially blues and gospel. Hard bop was *expressive.* It was sometimes bleak, often tormented, but always cathartic; and it was "bad" (sinister, menacing) in the sense that James Brown was "bad." In 1959, virtually every apartment building in areas like Harlem or the South Side of Chicago housed at least a few knowledgeable, serious jazz fans. Their historical awareness might not have extended very far back before the arrival of bebop, but they could eloquently debate the relative merits of tenor saxophonists like Harold Land and Booker Ervin or pianists like Bobby Timmons and Kenny Drew. Such fans usually had no more formal education than their neighbors who preferred the Drifters or Little Walter, but the quality of their interest was often different. They tended to be aficionados rather than casual listeners, and they thought of jazz as both "art" (in the Western sense of the term) *and* background music for partying, rather than as exclusively the latter.

Bars, of course, were crucial points of exposure to jazz, both live and on jukeboxes. Particularly common in ghettos—especially after Jimmy Smith hit the scene in the mid-fifties—were "soul jazz" combos featuring the likes of Lou Donaldson, Willis "Gator Tail" Jackson, Eddie "Lockjaw" Davis, Brother Jack McDuff, Jimmy McGriff, and Shirley Scott, as well as pianists like Ramsey Lewis, Gene Harris (of the Three Sounds), Red Garland, and Les McCann. In midwestern clubs (Manhattan below 96th Street was already in a more racially mixed, sophisticated class by itself in regard to live jazz), groups of this kind performed as often as "hard core" jazz combos led by musicians like Miles Davis, Art Blakey, and Horace Silver. Many bands were composed of local musicians who never achieved national recognition. As with salsa in the early 1990s, jazz in the 1950s was a good way to make a living and a lousy way to get rich. The concentration of independent labels in New York (Blue Note, Prestige, Riverside, and Savoy were the big four) also made it difficult for musicians to get a hearing elsewhere and acted as a magnet, sucking young jazzmen out of cities like Detroit and Philadelphia that had no recording industries to speak of.

A look at the jazz labels' singles lists reveals much about black taste during this period. Blue Note and Prestige each issued approximately three hundred 45-rpm singles between 1955 and 1970. Though both lists were stylistically broad, the tendency was definitely toward "listenable" and/or funky sounds: in other words, ballads and groove numbers. Blue Note leaned heavily toward the kind of playing done by the Three Sounds and by organists Big John Patton, Freddie Roach, Jimmy Smith, and Baby Face Willette; guitarists Kenny Burrell and Grant Green; saxophonists Lou Donaldson, Ike Quebec, and Stanley Turrentine; and trombonist Bennie Green. In second place were singles by hard-bop "stars" like Cannonball Adderley, Blakey, Silver, and Sonny Rollins. Musicians like Jackie McLean and vibist Bobby Hutcherson were far less generously represented (in McLean's case, for example, by "Greasy" from *New Soil*, and in Hutcherson's by "Ummh," from *San Francisco*). Both "Greasy" and "Ummh" are blues, "Greasy" being a kind of modified boogie-woogie and "Ummh" a slow grind with a heavy back beat. Still other artists, like Andrew Hill, were apparently judged too cerebral, even at their funkiest, to merit single releases.

The Prestige catalogue tells much the same story, but in a more extreme way. Bob Weinstock, who ran Prestige, was less committed to jazz as an "art form" than Blue Note's Alfred Lion and Frank Wolff. One result was that instead of just dominating Prestige's catalogue soul jazz is nearly the whole show: pianists Red Garland and Bobby Timmons; organists Chalres Earland, Richard "Groove" Holmes, Jack McDuff, Freddie Roach, Shirley Scott, Johnny "Hammond" Smith, and Larry Young; saxophonists Gene Ammons, Arnett Cobb,

Lockjaw Davis, Jimmy Forrest, Red Holloway, Gator Tail Jackson, and Houston Person; and guitarist Kenny Burrell, plus a very modest admixture of Miles Davis, John Coltrane, and the like.

In considering both lists, however, we should bear in mind that soul jazz musicians on the order of Gene Ammons, Kenny Burrell, and Jimmy Smith were outstanding jazzmen and that such others as Houston Person, Lockjaw Davis, and Ike Quebec were also very good indeed. Moreover, though for some musicians (like Gator Tail Jackson) soul jazz was the only context in which they felt comfortable, others (like Larry Young) could play demanding music (for example *Unity* on Blue Note) of great subtlety, attuned to a far more demanding aesthetic. One final point along these lines: although "groove numbers" were certainly the type most likely to end up on single releases, virtually all black musicians regarded them as simply one element of a varied repertoire.

According to Michael Cuscuna, arguably the world's leading authority on Blue Note and currently in charge of Capitol-EMI's Blue Note reissue program, the average sales for the company's singles were three thousand to jukebox operators, plus another thousand or so to individuals in black neighborhoods. Jukeboxes, in the 1950s and 1960s, were almost as important a means of exposure as radio. Joe Fields adds that singles (some of them truncated versions of tunes issued on LP in their complete form—for example, Cannonball Adderley's "Jive Samba," put out by Riverside in 1963) were sent out to black radio stations. Like virtually every other aspect of the music business, including distributors, record stores, and the companies themselves, black radio was then very different from what it is today. The voices of jazz dj's like Symphony Sid in New York and Daddy-O Daylie in Chicago filled the air of America's ghettos. Critic and musician Mark C. Gridley's comments on his early exposure to jazz give something of the flavor of radio fare at the time: "Growing up in Detroit, I heard hard bop more than any other style. In fact, during the early

1960s there was a radio station in Detroit that played almost nothing but hard bop. After arranging my high school and work schedules to enable me to hear as much of it as possible, I soon found that I could distinguish the sounds of Freddie Hubbard from Lee Morgan, Barry Harris from Tommy Flanagan, the Horace Silver Quintet from Art Blakey's Jazz Messengers, etc. So, even though my first jazz albums had been Duke Ellington reissues, I soon became very comfortable with hard bop, as well. (Eventually I managed to develop a tone quality in my tenor saxophone playing that resembled Joe Henderson's.)"[1]

How did jazz sell between 1950 and 1965? This question is not as easily answered as for other forms of black music, because jazz sales tend to accumulate over decades, not weeks. Thus, John Coltrane's *A Love Supreme*, one of the most popular jazz LPs ever with estimated sales of half a million, does not figure in *Billboard*'s lists of the Top 200 LPs between 1945 and 1972. Likewise, we find no Miles Davis records at all in *Billboard*'s listings before 1962, though by 1960 Miles possessed a townhouse in Manhattan, drove an expensive sports car, and dressed in custom-tailored Italian suits. Nonetheless, *Billboard*'s charts—both for LPs and for R & B singles—are worth examining. What we find, first of all, is that singles by Swing musicians (for instance Ella Fitzgerald's "Smooth Sailing," Lionel Hampton's "Rag Mop," and Johnny Hodges's "Castle Rock") still enjoyed brisk sales in the ghetto at the beginning of the 1950s. Modern jazz, no matter how much one stretches the term, is represented by only two entries during this period: King Pleasure's vocal versions of James Moody's "Moody's Mood for Love" and Gene Ammons's "Red Top." In addition, we find sides on the borderline between jazz and R & B (what would later be dubbed "soul jazz") like Illinois Jacquet's "Port of Rico" and Jimmy Forrest's "Night Train."

Very little jazz reached the R & B charts between 1953 and 1960, when jazz singles again began to appear there regularly. The reasons are diverse, but one of them is certainly that as

Swing began to sound old-fashioned to blacks and as bebop—never the stuff of jukebox hits—played itself out, the audience for jazz singles disintegrated. Meanwhile, however, a new generation of musicians returned to black music's popular roots. These musicians, in turn, made jazz more appealing to black listeners, who in the early 1960s responded by purchasing a new crop of hits. Some best-sellers of the period were Cannonball Adderley's "African Waltz," Ray Bryant's "Little Susie," Eddie Harris's "Exodus," Groove Holmes's "Misty," Ramsey Lewis's "The In Crowd," Gloria Lynne's version of Herbie Hancock's "Watermelon Man," Jimmy McGriff's rendition of Ray Charles's "I Got a Woman," Jimmy Smith's "Midnight Special," and Nancy Wilson's and Cannonball Adderley's "Save Your Love for Me." In all these cases, what we see is not so much popularity among jazz fans as crossover into R & B territory. Horace Silver, for instance—one of the era's biggest sellers on LP—is unrepresented, despite his numerous singles on Blue Note. Nonetheless, it was Silver and other prominent hard boppers who had created the atmosphere for such hit-makers, returning jazz to the hot, danceable rhythms and funky-butt emotions it had strayed from during the bebop era.

Billboard's top LP listings (not specifically R & B) also include a certain amount of jazz. As might be expected, hard bop and soul jazz predominate, though some of the material is more for "hard core" aficionados than that on the R & B charts, reflecting (among other things) the fact that jazz fans tend to buy LPs. Some serious jazz sides that made the Top 200 between 1960 and 1966 were Cannonball Adderley's *Jazz Workshop Revisited*; Gene Ammons's *Bad Bossa Nova*; Kenny Burrell's *The Tender Gender*; *Blue Bash*, featuring Burrell and Jimmy Smith; Miles Davis's *Someday My Prince Will Come* and *Seven Steps to Heaven*; Lou Donaldson's *Alligator Boogaloo*; Groove Holmes's *Soul Message*; Gloria Lynne's *I'm Glad There Is You*; Jack McDuff's *Live!*; Thelonious Monk's *Criss Cross*; Lee Morgan's *The Side-*

winder; Horace Silver's *Song for My Father;* six Jimmy Smith sides on Blue Note, the most successful being *Back at the Chicken Shack;* and *Nancy Wilson and Cannonball Adderley.*

Such LP charts, like the R & B listings, reflect a combination of weekly sales, airplay, and, in some cases, the clout of record companies advertising regularly and heavily in *Billboard.* In the case of independent jazz labels, this pressure was felt negatively. Blue Note, for example, never advertised in industry publications. According to Cuscuna's recollections, the label's all-time best-sellers were Lee Morgan's *The Sidewinder,* Horace Silver's *Song for My Father,* and Lou Donaldson's *Alligator Boogaloo,* all of which figured in *Billboard's* charts and sold something like a hundred thousand copies apiece over several years. Another big seller was Herbie Hancock's *Maiden Voyage,* which must have been slower to take off since it never made the charts. Like the title cut from *The Sidewinder,* used as background music for a Chrysler television spot, "Maiden Voyage" figured in a Fabergé commercial and, in fact, was listed on the master tape simply as "TV Jingle" and only christened later by Jean Hancock, Herbie's sister. Average initial sales for more straight-ahead hard-bop LPs like Jackie McLean's *New Soil,* again according to Cuscuna, ran from 6000 to 8000 copies, the break-even mark being about 2500. But, of course, many such records are still in print and selling well.

The world that generated them, however, has vanished into history books and recollections. I myself was lucky enough to experience the last few years of that world, and I can recall those glorious jukeboxes where Jimmy Smith, Miles Davis, and Cannonball Adderley rubbed shoulders with Martha Reeves, the Impressions, Muddy Waters, and Howlin' Wolf. The pervasiveness of jazz in the ghetto can be seen in the work of many R & B musicians formed during the 1960s—for example, that of the instrumentalists featured with Kool and the Gang or with Earth, Wind and Fire. Others, like saxophonist Wilton Felder and pianist Joe Sample of the Crusaders, actually were well-known jazz musicians. Still others, like Ray Charles, played jazz along with R & B, and even James Brown cut a few soul-jazz numbers (such as "Evil" on *James Brown Showtime*). All this occurred before, as Andrew Hill put it, "the music got separated."

How little "separated" the music was, at least in Chicago, can be seen from Clifford Jordan's memories of his introduction to jazz in the late 1940s. Like Hill, Jordan grew up on the city's South Side. We encountered him in the last chapter as Horace Silver's tenor saxophonist on *Further Explorations*. Since then, Jordan has evolved into one of the most expressive storytellers in jazz. In a way reminiscent of Swing titans like Benny Carter or Ben Webster, he has mellowed with the years, purifying his melodic conception without losing his fire: "When you'd go to a record store, they wouldn't have just thousands and thousands of pieces of material like you have now. They had the new Duke Ellington record, the new Count Basie, the new Louis Armstrong, so you could keep up with the music.

"I used to hear Eddie 'Lockjaw' Davis playing 'Doghouse' on the jukebox, and you could hear Coleman Hawkins's 'Body and Soul.' Yeah, all the jukeboxes, they had jazz, but nobody called it 'jazz' then. It was just music. It was just our music, folk music. So when I started playing saxophone, I went to the record store. I told the man behind the counter, I said, 'I'm interested in some saxophones. What records do you have with a saxophone on it?' So he pulled out Ben Webster, Charlie Ventura, Coleman Hawkins, Chu Berry, Lester Young, Johnny Hodges, so I bought a few records and listened to the guys. I got to Don Byas, but it was just easy to come by the music. They had two or three key record stores in the neighborhood."

Likewise, Jordan's own early professional experiences (from his first gig, a dance he played in 1947, to his arrival in New York City in 1956) exposed him to a wide variety of contexts and styles: "There were a few clubs that had the combos like Art Blakey and Bud Powell and Dizzy and Bird, Miles. They came through there, but there wasn't too many of those clubs around, and in the mainstream of the music at that time, all these so-called jazz musicians were playing commercial gigs. We had to play for a show, for dancers, so the only time we could play something that was really like the new type of music, bop as you would call it, would be when the band had a feature on the show, but a lot of times we had to play something like 'Flying Home,' which was a hit, and it was sort of like the house-rocking tenor solo, but people liked that.

"I played behind [blues singers] Willie Dixon, Arbee Stidham, Jump Jackson, Cool Breeze, all in Chicago. And I also played in Helen Coles's band, a woman who played drums from Texas. We did a little traveling to Buffalo and Peoria and places like that. Those were the kind of gigs you went on. Everybody wanted to hear some shake, rattle, and roll. I used to work a lot of strip gigs, for striptease, burlesque dancers, and we had a three-piece band. This was in Calumet City, and we would play behind a screen. So I had all these kinds of experiences."

Jordan's half-ironic comment on the influence of such work on his style reflects jazz musicians' mixed feelings about R & B gigs: "You try to clean house once in a while, but there's a lot of stuff that keeps coming out."

Just as most major rhythm-and-blues singers started out in church choirs, virtually all the best hard boppers paid at least some R & B dues. Even Jackie McLean, who identified himself early on as a bebopper and was sponsored by Bud Powell, Thelonious Monk, Charlie Parker, and Miles Davis, had experiences parallel to Jordan's: "I played in rhythm and blues bands when I went to North Carolina in 1953 to try to go to school again, and I stayed down there for a year, and yeah, it helped me. It influenced me. I was playing with a group in Greensboro. Danny Richmond at that time was playing saxophone, and it was him and myself and T. J. Anderson, who was a jazz and classical composer for Tufts University. He was there at that time, so we played around in the local clubs and

rhythm and blues bands, the ABA Club and different clubs in
the city, backing up singers and playing blues, most of the time
in one key all night depending on who was the bandleader.
There was one saxophone player who used to play everything
in E-flat. When he was the bandleader we played blues in E-flat
all night, and I used to walk the bar with him, battle with him. I
worked with him a great deal. The first record I made was not
with Miles. I made a rhythm-and-blues piece with Charlie
Singleton's band called 'Camel Walkin' where I played baritone sax, no solo."

It was also in North Carolina that McLean was first exposed
to gospel music, an experience that remained semi-dormant in
him until his stint with Charles Mingus in the late 1950s:
"When I heard it, I heard it as a child in church, and especially
when I would go visit my grandmother in North Carolina. She
went to a traditional Pentecostal kind of Baptist church, tent
meetings in small churches that really got into the heavy
aspects of the rhythm and the people passing out, feeling the
spirit and the whole thing, so I saw that as a child, and I never
really put that in place again and put it into my music, even
though it was there unconsciously, till Mingus's band, which
gave me a kind of resurgence of that, because he used to like to
shout and play shout music and music that was closely related
to the church, so my experience with Mingus might have
helped me."

Thus, when McLean describes the differences between bebop and hard bop, he is also describing his own evolution and
the elements of his style: "Certainly Charlie Parker kept all
the roots there. I mean, he was definitely a blues player and a
lot of the music that he composed was structured on the blues
form, and yet there was another kind of gospel feeling, a funk
kind of feeling if I can use that term, that came into the music
in the mid-fifties with Horace [Silver] and some of the guys
that were thinking along these lines. I certainly, myself,
thought along heavy blues lines, blues feeling, and my concept
of it, so I just think it had more of a gospel feeling to it, a

sanctified feeling to it mixed with all the other ingredients that Bird, Bud, Thelonious gave us."

For some musicians steeped in the bebop tradition, with its cult of defiant innovation, interest in the "roots" of black music—blues and gospel—only awakened gradually. Indeed, McLean implies as much in his comments on gospel. Pianist Walter Bishop, Jr., who along with McLean formed part of New York City's second generation of beboppers and went on to play with Charlie Parker, recalls that: "My generation rebelled against that simplistic music coming or even blues. I couldn't even play the blues till later years. I didn't want to know about the blues because to me the generation of the blues was representative of the subservient black. We'd graduated from that.

"I had to reach a certain level of confidence, of being secure in my power to know that it wasn't a drag to play the blues. Then I could let that go and relax enough to absorb some of the roots. Before that I would have been afraid to even get into that because they would think that was all I could do. Bebop was a social statement as well as music because the whole thing evolved and changed. I mean the generation that were before mine absorbed the pain and humiliation of the fact that they had to be buffoons. They made it possible for my generation to get over on pure virtuosity and ability, so I remember when I first started making professional gigs people would look at me: 'Why don't you smile, boy? Ain't you happy?' I said: "Smile? What's that got to do with it? I'm serious about this.' But I got just a little taste of what my predecessors dealt with, that they couldn't be accepted as artists. They had to be buffoons."

In the late fifties, the cult of "soul" was also connected to a rise in militancy among black musicians, and the blues became a symbol of racial pride rather than of oppression. Nat Hentoff quotes a "young Negro trombonist from Detroit who came close to starvation during several months of trying to establish himself in New York, but nourished himself on the belief that the jazz at least had the authenticity that many white musicians lacked. His playing had 'soul,' and, as he once explained the term warily to a white jazz critic, 'that soul only comes from certain kinds of experiences, and only we—you know who I mean—go through what you need to have the kind of soul that makes real jazz.' "[2]

Hentoff goes on to say that "This renewed reverence for 'church' feeling and 'funky' blues by Negro musicians has turned into one of the most commercial jazz commodities in the past fifteen years, judging by record sales and club appearances of the neo-gospel boppers. 'I think most of that soul music is now being manufactured rather than felt,' said a Harlem record store owner, 'but at least this is one time in jazz history when the Negroes are popularizing their own music. It would take a lot of courage for Stan Kenton or Shorty Rodgers to call one of their albums *The Soul Brothers*.' "[3]

If "soul" was both (in Jackie McLean's words) "rooted in what Ray Charles sings, blues and gospel music" and a banner of racial self-affirmation, it was certainly a marketing device during hard bop's heyday. Nonetheless, in their emphasis on expressiveness, physicality, and "funk" (a word whose original meaning—strong bodily odors, especially sexual ones—expresses its earthiness), hard boppers restored jazz to popularity in black neighborhoods. Art Blakey, one of hard bop's most eloquent spokesmen, summed it up recently: "Fire! That's what people want. You know, music is supposed to wash away the dust of everyday life . . . You're supposed to make them turn around, pat their feet. That's what *jazz* is about . . . Play with fire; play from the heart, not from your brain. You got to know how to utilize, make the two meet. You just don't play out of the top of your head, or play down to the people. I think you should play *to* the people."

Jazz and Bohemia

The period between 1945 and 1965 was an extraordinarily creative one in New York City and—in a more dispersed way—

in other parts of the United States as well. New York, however, was the magnet that drew artists of all sorts. Space was still cheap in lower Manhattan. America's far-flung universities had little interest in recruiting experimentalists-in-residence, and the one serious exception to this rule, Black Mountain College, folded in the fifties, sending much of its teaching staff and student body to New York as well. Bohemian Manhattan was an intimate, small-scale scene: a band of outsiders easily recognizable by their dress and demeanor. Groups that later would seem diametrically opposed or at least very different—for example, the Beats and the "New York School" of poetry—rubbed elbows amiably and frequented the same bars and jazz clubs. Being few in number, they were obliged to stick together; in Eisenhower's blandly conformist America, all weirdos were brothers until the opposite was proven. In addition, artists shared an exhilaration born of their recent liberation from Europe. The old American colonial complex—a sense of being on the periphery of things, still strong among the modernists of the 1920s—had been swept away by the triumph of abstract expressionism, by William Carlos Williams's appropriation of American speech as a basis for new poetry, and, of course, by jazz, the American art form *par excellence*.

Needless to say, not all artists frequented bars and jazz joints, but a remarkable number did. The abstract expressionists—Jackson Pollock, Willem de Kooning, Franz Kline, and others—were hard drinkers and inveterate hangers-out. One of them, Larry Rivers, was also an accomplished jazz saxophonist and served as a point of intersection between the worlds of painting and jazz. The Beats also spent a lot of time in night spots. For the New York School (Kenneth Koch, John Ashbery, and others), a key connection with jazz was Frank O'Hara, whose best-known poem, a poignantly oblique homage to Billie Holiday, is entitled "The Day Lady Died." Judith Malina's and Julian Beck's Living Theatre, with its mixture of raw psychodrama and dreamy pacifism, sponsored poetry readings

at its headquarters on 14th Street and featured Jackie McLean
and hard-bop pianist Freddie Redd in its production of Jack
Gelber's play *The Connection.*

Almost anyone's account of the era includes both this heady
mixture of scenes and the centrality of jazz as an artistic model
and jazz clubs as meeting places. Ron Sukenick's *Down and
In: Life in the Underground,* a combined study and memoir
covering the period from 1945 through the eighties, describes
the clientele and atmosphere at the Five Spot in the late fifties:
"If the painting seemed more consciously American after
1950, the uniquely native American art form, jazz, became,
through the fifties, more central than ever for underground
artist of all kinds. It came together at the Five Spot, a bar
on Cooper Square where the brothers Iggie and Joe Termini
hosted a basically flophouse clientele until the artist started
coming in during the mid-fifties. Painters like Grace Hartigan,
Al Leslie, David Smith, de Kooning became habitués. Larry
Rivers, the painter, played jazz there, poets read poetry to jazz,
and avant-garde film makers even showed their films to jazz.
Writers like Kerouac, Frank O'Hara, and Kenneth Koch moved
in, and finally the great jazzmen themselves came down to
play—Charlie Mingus, Sonny Rollins, Cecil Taylor, Thelonious Monk, Ornette Coleman."[4]

In response to a question about which jazz musicians downtown artists and intellectuals were friendliest with, the
painter Emilio Cruz (who also writes poetry and plays jazz
drums) gave this description of the scene: "In the case of Jackie
McLean, I would think that if he was around the Living
Theatre crowd, he was friendly with Judith Malina and Julian
Beck and that crowd, and a number of interesting people in
that company. Also Cubby Selby; we all called him Cubby. I
never knew his real name was Hubert Selby, Jr., until his book
[*Last Exit to Brooklyn*] came out. Paul Blackburn, the poet,
who was a good friend of mine, knew a lot of those people. Bob
Thompson the painter, Allen Ginsberg at times, Bob Kaufman

the poet, some of the Black Mountain poets. Rollins lived downtown and knew a number of artists, though he was very solitary.

"Others who were there not just because it was cool but because they had a deep interest in the music were [Amiri] Baraka and Larry Rivers. [Rivers] was a friend of Zoot Sims, Stan Getz. I know he considers himself as serious a saxophone player as he does a painter. During that period I lived on Jefferson Street, down by the river. Pepper Adams lived in that building underneath me. In fact, he was the only one in the building who had heat. He had a gas heater, so in the winter when he was on the road I was a lot colder than when he was there. Donald Byrd used to come by a lot because they had that band together at that time. Jefferson Street was south of East Broadway, maybe southeast, not that far from where the old Fulton Fish Market was. That's all changed now. I don't even know whether that street exists anymore. Ed Blackwell used to come by that building too.

"That was a period, in my life, when a lot of things were integrated. Jazz was integrated within artists' lives. A lot of people lived in lofts, and oftentimes the musicians might not have lived in lofts themselves, but they would come over there (at least on the Lower East Side) to play, to rehearse a band, so there were a lot of connections because of that. That connection would then extend what a person's capacity was, so that one person might learn more about music, another person might learn more about painting or poetry, and I knew a number of musicians who were interested in learning about all of it. Like I'm friends with Grachan Moncur III. I was his drummer last year at his workshop in New Jersey. He used to come visit my studio all the time. There was a lot of openness between various people. Herbie Lewis, the bass player, he lived around the corner. He was a neighbor of mine, so we spent a lot of time together. Miles . . . I know numbers of people from the beat generation who were friends with Miles, like Allen Ginsberg, Jack Kerouac, Robert Frank the photographer. So there was an integration of lots of the arts. The beat generation spent much of their lives in clubs.

"Now one of the things that it's very important to understand is that there weren't thousands of people involved in the arts in those days, so when you would walk down the street in New York City, you would look at somebody and you would recognize them instantly as an artist, and you would immediately find that you had some kind of rapport, and there's another thing. I can't speak for right now, but there was youth. Youth reaches out. There's one thing that was consistent in all the artists in New York City at that time. They were reaching out for new things, new ways of expressing themselves. They were attempting to discover new values. Those values were not necessarily ones that were supported by the society at large, so there was this that they had in common. Another thing was that there was an attempt to break down racism, and politically there was a sense of hope that America could arrive at a higher moral state. So racism was something that in that world was frowned upon."

What did jazz *mean* to those experimental artists who took it most seriously? Part of the answer, as Sukenick indicates, has to do with its American qualities, also underlined by Hettie Jones, author of *Big Star Fallin' Mama*, a study of black female vocalists from Bessie Smith to Aretha Franklin: "I think jazz was the music they [downtown bohemian types] felt closest to, the way someone feels close to music that's part of the zeitgeist. It was American. There's that whole idea that abstract expressionist art was the first truly American art movement; and those people saw themselves as an avant-garde in what they were trying to do. It was a shared feeling that they were all part of a changing American art scene."

Jazz was also influential in its improvisational freedom and structural openness, as Allen Ginsberg indicates in his description of jazz's relationship with his poem "Howl": "In the dedication of 'Howl' I said 'spontaneous bop prosody.' And the ideal, for Kerouac, and for John Clellon Holmes and for me also, was the legend of Lester Young playing through something like sixty-nine to seventy choruses of 'Lady Be Good,' you know, mounting and mounting and building and building more and more intelligence into the improvisation as chorus after chorus went on . . . riding on chorus after chorus and building and building so it was a sort of ecstatic orgasmic expostulation of music. So there was the idea of chorus after chorus building to a climax, which was the notion of part one of 'Howl,' with each verse being like a little saxophone obbligato or a little saxophone chorus, as though what I was doing was combining the long line of Christopher Smart, the eighteenth-century poet, with notions of the repeated jazz or blues chorus, till it comes to a climax, probably in the verse 'ah, Carl, while you are not safe I am not safe.' And then there's a sort of a coda from then on."

Ginsberg also claims jazz as an important model for his work and that of his contemporaries: "The whole point of modern poetry, dance, improvisation, performance, prose even, music, was the element of improvisation and spontaneity and open form, or even a fixed form improvisation on that form, like say you have a blues chorus and you have spontaneous improvisations, so in 'Howl' or 'Kaddish' or any of the poems that have a listeny style, 'who did this, who did that, who did this,' you start out striking a note, 'who,' and then you improvise, and that's the basic form of the list poem or, in anaphora, when you return to the margins in the same phrase, 'Or ever the golden bowl be broken or the silver cord be loosed or the pitcher be broken at the fountain,' as in the Bible or as in some of Walt Whitman's catalogues or in Christopher Smart's 'Rejoice in the Lamb' poem or the surrealist example of André Breton's free union, 'my wife with the platypus's egg, my wife with the eyes of this, my wife with that and that . . .'

"It [jazz] was a model for the dadaists and it was a model for the surrealists and it was a model for Kerouac and a model for me and a model for almost everybody, in the sense that it was partly a model and partly a parallel experiment in free form.

The development of poetics, as well as jazz and painting, seems to be chronologically parallel, which is to say you have fixed form, which then evolves toward more free form where you get let loose from this specific repeated rhythm and improvise the rhythms even, where you don't have a fixed rhythm, as in bebop the drum became more of a soloist in it too. So you find that in painting, the early de Koonings have a motif or a theme, the woman or something like that, but it gets more and more open, less dependent on the theme, and in poetry, where you have less and less dependence on the original motifs and more and more John Ashberyesque improvisational free form flowing without even a subject matter, though I always kept a subject matter like the old funky blues myself. It was partly a parallel development within each discipline: painting, poetry, music. There were innovators who opened up the thing after Einstein, so to speak—you know, relative measure, as Williams said—which is in a sense something that happened with bebop: not the fixed measure but a relative measure. It was both inter-influential and parallel, also integrating."

If jazz opened up Ginsberg to "the awakening of Afric slave sensibility, of black sensibility, black funk as distinct from white, clean Doris Day ethic, and mind funk instead of well-combed, academic, button-down poetry," some jazz musicians, as Cruz comments, were also "interested in learning about *all* of it." Many, however, were not. After all, there were still plenty of clubs in black neighborhoods until the mid-sixties, and for lots of jazzmen, a job downtown—at Café Bohemia, the Village Vanguard, the Five Spot, or wherever—was just another gig. When I asked Walter Bishop, Jr., about his take on the lower Manhattan avant-garde twenty-five years ago, he replied that at the time he'd "had blinkers on," that for him it had been "bebop or bust"—in other words, that he'd had no artistic interests outside jazz.

Others, however, like Jackie McLean, were intensely curious about the worlds around them. McLean found his way into painting and (to a lesser degree) literature through his "friendship with guys who were doing this, for instance Harvey Cropper, who was the first painter that I knew. He was the one that introduced me to Bartók, to a lot of painters, the style of Cézanne. He introduced me to Hieronymus Bosch and that opened another world. That was the painter that had the greatest influence on me, Bosch, because my world was so horrible at that time that I could understand his paintings. I could look at the horror in some of his paintings and feel it when I was sick [from lack of narcotics], and then when I met Bob Thompson in 'sixty-one and we became very close, I learned a great deal about painting from Bob, being around him and talking about the music and painting and what not. And of course Leroi Jones was around in those days, and we were all hanging in the Village together during that time."

McLean's period (1959–1963) with the Living Theatre also widened his interests. During these years he evolved from a promising journeyman bebopper, described by Steve Lacy in *The Jazz Review* in 1959 as having "the most rhythmic vitality and, so far, the least discipline"[5] of major saxophonists, into the brilliant experimentalist we hear on records from the early sixties like *Let Freedom Ring* and *Evolution*. The intensity of McLean's experience in the Living Theatre comes through in his reminiscences about the troupe: "I thought they were great people. I thought they were people who were looking far into the future, for a better way. You had to love them to be with them, because the Living Theatre was like a big commune. Mostly everybody lived together, ate together, and were together working out each person's problems. I didn't live with them because I had my wife and kids, but I was part of it because certainly I lived with them when we left New York, when we went to Europe.

"It was weird because the day that we left, there was a big snowstorm in Manhattan and all the transportation was stopped. It was the biggest snowstorm I ever saw. The night before there was no snow. I wake up the next day, we're

supposed to leave for Europe, and the phone rings. The guy says
'Jackie, this is Hacker.' So I said 'Yeah, I know. We're not going.
We can't get there,' so he says 'No. An ambulance is coming to
get you. We had to hire ambulances to pick everybody up.' I
said 'Jesus Christ, man,' and I was so strung out, so sick, so my
wife walked me to the hallway and we stood there with my
bags and my horn and my children and this ambulance came
and I went downstairs and put my bags in the ambulance and
two arms came out and helped me in. We went and picked up
the next guy and went to where the ship was, the Queen
Elizabeth, and the whole cast was coming in in ambulances, a
sick group coming in ambulances, but when I say 'sick,' I mean
sick in terms of having a better understanding of what life is
supposed to be about. They were very hip people, Judith and
Julian and the whole crowd. They were humanists. They were
all into every aspect of art and their idea of theater was brand-
new in terms of how they wanted to present it."

Bohemianism, of course, is not all purity and innocence.
Ever since the concept was invented, it has also meant pleasure, doing what feels good, and rebellion, surreptitious or
open, against constraints of all sorts. Another aspect of jazz's
attraction for Village types was its renegade connotations.
Again in Emilio Cruz's words: "Jazz became the heretic art
form. What we call 'gutbucket' has not to do so much with the
guts or the bucket but it has to do with heresy. So what is
unique in modern culture is the heretic form. Everything that
is created, in truth, outside of the sciences which deal directly
with a mechanistic culture, comes out of heresy, so that Allen
Ginsberg was involved in a kind of heresy. Charlie Parker was
also involved in a kind of heresy. There is the idea of violation,
and that violation would attract those people that were searching for that heretic tradition."

At one extreme, such heresy and will to violation leads
artists to flirt with or embrace the most perilous vices. While
jazz was the banner of a kind of fresh and Edenic newness in
the arts, it was also a path into the lower depths, as implied by

Sukenick's comment on underground rebels of the 1950s: "Where are you in the mid-fifties? Are you fighting your way up the heart-burning ladder of career, or have you finally decided there's no place to go but down? Burned out into a dead-end underground. Into the shadow world emblemized above all by Bebop. Digging Bop is one of the main ways subterraneans can express their cultural radicalism."[6]

Jazz's "shadow world" was the kingdom of the hipster, a stereotype partly mythical and partly based on reality, but far more cynical than the flower-child, love-and-peace "hippies" of the late 1960s. A furtive, jive-talking sociopath, the hipster was supposedly alert only to his own whims and his craving for intense experiences. In "The White Negro" (1957), which remains an intriguing and annoying essay, Norman Mailer wrote that "the source of Hip is the Negro for he has been living on the margin between totalitarianism and democracy for two centuries. But the presence of Hip as a working philosophy in the sub-worlds of American life is probably due to jazz, and its knifelike entrance into culture, its subtle but so penetrating influence on an avant-garde generation—that postwar generation of adventurers who (some consciously, some by osmosis) had absorbed the lessons of disillusionment and disgust of the twenties, the depression, and the war."[7]

Mailer's piece drew heavy criticism from those in the jazz world who read it. They faulted it for presenting a series of caricatures. So it does—not necessarily much of a defect in an essay whose tone is so exaggerated and polemical anyway— but many of them fit, at least partly, the jazz scene at that time.

What Mailer perhaps did not emphasize enough was the centrality of drugs and particularly heroin among hipsters. As Leonard Feather noted in "Jazz in American Society" (published as a foreword to his *Encyclopedia of Jazz*, 1960): "A serious effect of the use of drugs, quite apart from the medical, is its creation of a sub-society in which all the users are 'hip' and the rest of the world is 'square.'"[8] "Hip talk" itself was partly a necessary camouflage for discussions of drugs, what

Mailer called "the cunning of their language, the abstract ambiguous alternatives in which from the danger of their oppression they learned to speak ('Well now, man, like I'm looking for a cat to turn me on . . .')."[9]

The mysterious, hedonistic yet cooled-out universe of junkies in pursuit of what Balzac called "quiet, inner enjoyment," and their profound alienation from society as a whole—an alienation often compounded by race—were perceived as deeply attractive by some bohemians. Even as fire-breathing a revolutionary as Amiri Baraka, who has often railed against drugs, surrenders to their sinister glamour when describing (in *The Autobiography of Leroi Jones*) his use of heroin with painter Bob Thompson in the early sixties—this despite the fact that Thompson's very promising career was cut short by an overdose: "I walked all the way back to Avenue C, not to see Lucia, but to find a friend of mine, Bob Thompson, a black painter. Bob lived in a huge loft on Clinton Street. He was there with a couple of bohemians, getting high, shooting heroin. I didn't know he used it, but he was sending one of the bohemians out to cop. I dropped some money in the mitt and meanwhile used some of Bob's 'smack' and we took off together, down, down, and right here! Bob and I were a number after that."[10]

There can be no doubt that heroin use was widespread among jazz musicians. As Leonard Feather pointed out in "Jazz in American Society": "Of the 23 individuals listed as winners in a recent *Down Beat* poll, at least nine were known narcotics users, five of them with a record of arrest and conviction. The proportion is even greater among proponents of certain types of jazz, notably 'hard bop,' whose principal soloists include an alarmingly high percentage with police records as heroin addicts."[11]

The percentage of junkies among hard boppers was indeed alarming and is the main reason why so few of them are alive today. Why did so many get hooked? It has often been said that heroin cannot improve one's music. This is probably true, and yet . . . what made Edith Piaf and Billie Holiday so haunting, and in such similar ways? Heroin certainly induces relaxation, and with it a kind of detached lucidity, as suggested by Nat Hentoff in *The Jazz Life* when he quotes "one very successful musician, who compared taking heroin to '. . . going into a closet. It lets you concentrate and takes you away from everything. Heroin is a working drug, like the doctor who took it because he had a full schedule so he could work better. It lets me concentrate on my sound.'"[12]

Still another standard explanation—discrimination, lack of recognition, or whatever you want to call it—was summarized by Walter Bishop, Jr., who, like Clifford Jordan and Jackie McLean, is an ex-junkie: "The whole thing is when you've got a whole lot to express and you can't express it, so it's a form of self-medication, just trying to cool yourself out. It's the pain of being so creative and not having avenues to express it or having your work considered less than important that could drive a man to many things."

Perhaps, after all, hard bop's frequent combination of tough street attitudes and somber melancholy *did* have something to do with heroin. In any case, it was central to many of the school's members; hard-living, fast-burning creative torches who appeared in remarkable profusion and all too often were snuffed out at their brightest moments. It is to some of these— lyricists, soul-jazz specialists, and tormented poets of anguish in the manner of Billie Holiday—that we shall now turn our attention.

5

THE LYRICISTS

Brown, Farmer, Golson, Gryce, Jones, and Associates

In Mark C. Gridley's *Jazz Styles: History and Analysis,* a textbook designed for use in history of jazz courses, we find trumpeter Art Farmer, pianists Tommy Flanagan and Barry Harris, and composers Benny Golson and Gigi Gryce classified as "hard boppers."[1] Such musicians are indeed to be associated with hard bop for two reasons. First, they often collaborated with hard boppers; and second, the very breadth and diversity of hard bop helped their styles to develop. But the decisive quality they share with each other is their gentle, thoughtful elegance. The distance between them and the school's rawer exponents can be seen in Barry Harris's account of a run-in with Blue Note Records' Alfred Lion, who favored more high-voltage sounds: "I made a record with Lee Morgan, *The Sidewinder,* for Blue Note, and I went to the Blue Note man and asked him why didn't he give me a record date—he said I played too beautiful. So I thanked him and walked out."[2]

"Beautiful," of course, is one of the vaguest words around. But Harris's meaning—tunefulness and lyricism—is clear enough. It brings us close to what Tadd Dameron meant when he told his band in 1953: "When I write something it's with beauty in mind. It has to swing, sure, but it has to be beautiful." The lesson was not wasted, for those listening included Golson and Gryce, Tadd's main heirs (along with Jimmy Heath) in writing richly voiced, vibrantly melodic modern-jazz originals.

Such beauty was also what bebop trumpeter Freddie Webster had in mind. As harmonically sophisticated as Dizzy Gillespie and other jaggedly multi-noted beboppers, Webster played more sparely, emphasizing melody and a fat sound, dark yet brassy, that Gillespie called "the best I ever heard."[3] Webster's career was tragically short. He died in 1947 at the age of thirty, leaving behind only a handful of recorded solos from which those of us who never heard him in person must reconstruct his style. His legacy, however, turned out to be as important as Gillespie's or Fats Navarro's. Webster has been frequently cited as an early influence on Miles Davis. And in 1984, nearly forty years after Webster's death, Art Farmer described the tonal quality of his own playing: "I wouldn't say it was a completely original sound, I've heard similarities in other musicians, like Shorty Baker, Miles Davis, Freddie Webster, Benny Bailey . . . a broad sound with a little bit of edge when you want it."[4]

Webster, then, along with Dameron and swing pianist Teddy Wilson, whose delicate, filigreed style colored Hank Jones's and Tommy Flanagan's music, was another major influence on hard-bop lyricists. Apart from Davis, Webster's best-known disciple was Art Farmer. Born in 1928, Farmer grew up in Phoenix, Arizona. In 1945, he and his twin brother Addison (an excellent bassist who died in 1963 just after completing his studies at the Juilliard School of Music) spent their summer vacation in Los Angeles. Their holiday coincided with the eruption of bebop. In an interview with *Coda* magazine's Bill Smith, Farmer recalled the feeling of shared discovery among young musicians: "There was so much going on compared to Phoenix that we decided we would just stay there. And we met all the guys around. Things were quite open. There was a lot of enthusiasm. Everybody was trying to learn. There was a general sharing of knowledge. I remember Charlie Parker came there with Dizzy and he decided to stay. We were all in the same clique, but he would walk the street with us at night too. Looking for a place to play. If a job came we'd take it and if it didn't we'd just go and jam and wait until the next gig came."[5]

Farmer spent his senior year of high school in L.A. After working with Horace Henderson and Floyd Ray, he went on the road with Johnny Otis's jazz and R & B group. But after four months in Otis's outfit, Farmer's lip gave out and he was fired: "I was first trumpet in the band, with no previous experience, and I was doing it wrong. Freddie Webster told me to see a guy named Grupp, and he was a very warm and human person. I thought I'd better stay in New York and study and get myself straightened out. I worked as a porter in a theater and studied with Maurice Grupp every day."[6]

After this period of "woodshedding," Farmer joined Jay McShann's band (another ensemble combining jazz and blues) and worked his way back to the West Coast. By now his style and technique had evolved to the point where he could hold his own with California's leading beboppers: musicians like trumpeter Benny Bailey (who remains one of his favorites); saxophonists Sonny Criss, Teddy Edwards, Dexter Gordon, Wardell Gray, and Frank Morgan; and pianist Hampton Hawes. Though these associations were not very lucrative ("I played every chance I got . . . They were hard times then. And at that time I was still trying to learn. But I was one of many. There must have been a million guys there"[7]), they led to Farmer's first jazz recording date: a sextet session led by Gray. Here Farmer's style is still embryonic, though on "April Skies," a medium-tempo cut on which he plays with a mute, one can glimpse the future artisan of carefully crafted lines. Two of the faster tracks ("Bright Boy" and "Farmer's Market") also feature trumpet solos. These are of a more conventionally boppish order, yet here too, in Farmer's pure, ringing tone and attention to timbre, one can glimpse his future development.

In 1952 Farmer joined Lionel Hampton's big band, which also included, at various times during his stay, Benny Bailey, Clifford Brown, and composers Golson, Gryce, and Quincy Jones. That must have been one hell of a band! More's the pity that, having assembled such a brilliant group of young jazzmen, Hampton, anxious to please a public that expected him to repeat his past glories, didn't allow them more freedom. Nonetheless, both Gryce and Farmer deemed the orchestra the best Hamp had ever led. As an incubator for hard bop's more lyrical stylists, it was extraordinarily productive, as important a nucleus of major talents as any since the birth of modern jazz. We can get some idea of what it sounded like from a series of sessions recorded for French Vogue during a 1953 European tour. The tunes, Brian Blevins reports in his liner notes, "were provided mainly by Gigi Gryce and Quincy Jones (the arrangements had probably been charted for the Hampton band but unused by that organization)." These arrangements are an intriguing mixture of such Swing big-band approaches as the sleek, bouncingly Basieish theme of "Keepin' Up with Jonesy," Dameronian tints, and orchestral ideas taken from scores by Johnny Carisi, Gil Evans, Gerry Mulligan, and others that ended up on Miles Davis's *Birth of the Cool* LP. The richness of the voicings and secondary themes, the tight ensembles, and the constant play of surging, shifting orchestrated accompaniments all help create some of our finest examples of big-band modern jazz.

These sessions, as their collective title (*Clifford Brown in Paris*) suggests, featured Brownie, Hampton's fiery young trumpeter. Brown also cut a ten-inch LP for Blue Note in 1953 featuring charts by Gryce and Jones, but he soon veered off in another direction, playing first with Art Blakey and Horace Silver and then with Max Roach and Sonny Rollins. It was Art Farmer, heard only in ensemble passages on the Paris dates, who went on to collaborate more extensively with Gryce and later with Golson as well.

Gryce, born in 1927 and raised in Hartford, Connecticut, studied at that city's Julius Hart School of Music, then at Boston Conservatory with Alan Hovhaness, and finally in Paris, on a Fulbright fellowship, with Nadia Boulanger and Arthur Honegger. An altoist and flutist as well as a composer and arranger, he attracted attention as early as 1951 through tunes like "Yvette," "Wildwood," and "Mosquito Knees," all recorded by Stan Getz. In the early fifties, Gryce also contributed originals to record dates led by J.J. Johnson ("Capri"), Howard McGhee ("Shabozz"), Max Roach ("Glowworm"), and Clifford Brown ("Brownskin" and "Hymn of the Orient"). Gryce's association with Farmer on records (like that with Brownie) dates from 1953: a session for Prestige featuring Quincy Jones originals but including a Gryce composition entitled "Up in Quincy's Room." Like the entire web of relationships and affinities we've been discussing (Jones–Brown; Brown–Gryce; Jones–Gryce; Gryce–Golson; Golson–Farmer; and to complicate things further, during that same 1953 European tour, Brown and Farmer co-led a record date, with scores by Jones, in Sweden!), the Gryce–Farmer connection was cemented in Hamp's orchestra. In the fall of 1953, after returning to Manhattan, Gryce and Farmer settled near each other: Farmer on West 55th Street and Gryce on West 52nd. In 1954 they co-led a band at the Tiajuana Club in Baltimore and also recorded for Prestige, but the Farmer–Gryce quintet didn't crystallize as a regular unit until 1955. At that time, Gryce outlined some of the ensemble's perspectives: "What we've done on records so far is just the nucleus. We want to experiment with different approaches. Above all, we intend to maintain a richness, a beauty of melodic line no matter how odd the harmonies underneath might be. We want our music to be understood."[8] Later in the same interview, Gryce went on to say: "We're not restricting ourselves to the traditional 32-bar choruses. We'll write and play in the framework of any number of bars that will best express our ideas. Nor do we want to be stuck with the usual pattern whereby the piano opens with four or eight bars, then everybody states the theme, followed by each man blowing a chorus on a basic set of changes."[9]

Gryce's wish to produce a fresh sound, innovative but not aridly "experimental," was realized in three 1955 recording sessions: two with a quintet co-led by him and Farmer for Prestige (*When Farmer Met Gryce* and *Art Farmer Quintet*) and one with a nonet for the Signal label (reissued on *Signals*, Savoy). All three, of course, feature Gryce originals, many of which (for example, "Evening in Casablanca," a forty-six-bar theme, and "Nica's Tempo," which is forty-four bars long) do not fit standard Tin Pan Alley formulas. The harmonies are original and more impressionistic than had been habitual in bebop. Secondary themes, arranged accompanying figures, and motifs used to launch new solos abound, adding textural variety. On the nonet tracks, Gryce uses constantly shifting tonal colors and instrumental combinations to create dense orchestrations, yet his themes are so light and airy, so swinging and songlike, that they never bog down. Particularly notable are three ballads: "The Infant's Song," "Evening in Casablanca," and "In a Meditating Mood," among the most poignant compositions in modern jazz. Gryce's tunes are perfect foils for Farmer's solos, which highlight his slightly sour tone and his probing, off-center lines. These solos methodically explore each tune's harmonic interstices, yet their brooding air keeps them from sounding excessively deliberate. Together, they bear out both Farmer's statement that "I want each note to count"[10] and bassist Sam Jones's description of him as "one of the most lyrical trumpet players in the world—I mean he really knows how to play a melody with *feeling*. If you don't have what's needed to project from the stage to the audience then I think you're just wasting your time."[11]

The Farmer–Gryce quintet stayed together until June 1956, when it disbanded, a casualty of sporadic gigs and consequent problems in maintaining a stable rhythm section familiar with Gryce's book. Gryce began free-lancing and eventually formed the Jazz Lab quintet with trumpeter Donald Byrd, while Farmer joined Horace Silver's combo (see Chapter 3).

Gryce continued to be an active presence on the New York jazz scene, often in tandem with Benny Golson, whose reputation as the author of memorable, dark-hued originals and Dameron-influenced arrangements increasingly paralleled Gryce's. The two collaborated on Lee Morgan's *City Lights* (Blue Note) and Dizzy Gillespie's *The Greatest Trumpet of Them All* (Verve), while Golson's recordings under his own name featured not only his own tunes but such Gryce originals as "You're Not the Kind," "Calgary," "Capri," and "Reunion." Golson has been explicit about Dameron's influence on his work: "Tadd's music really ignited the spark for me. After hearing things like "Our Delight" and "Lady Bird," I had more of a definite goal. I wanted to do more than play the tenor sax. I wanted to write."[12] In addition, Golson's first professional gig, after completing his schooling at Howard University, was with Bullmoose Jackson's R & B band, which included Philly Joe Jones, bassist Jymie Merritt, and Dameron as pianist and sometime arranger. A friendship between the two composers sprang up, and Golson decided to dedicate a tune to Tadd: "I didn't title it, because I didn't know if Tadd would approve. After the band played it a couple of times, Tadd said he liked it. Then I told him that I'd written it for him and asked him if it would be all right to call it 'Shades of Dameron.' He was pleased, and so was I."[13]

Later Golson played tenor in the Dameron band that included Gryce and Clifford Brown. His stately, dignified tribute to the trumpeter, "I Remember Clifford," has become a modern jazz classic. In the mid-fifties, Golson contributed charts to Lee Morgan's first three Blue Note record dates, played in and wrote for Dizzy Gillespie's big band, and co-starred with Morgan in the Jazz Messengers, to which he contributed such tunes as the sassy, light-tipping "Along Came Betty" and the

hard-driving "Are You Real?" and "Blues March." At the same
time, Golson's and Farmer's paths crossed on numerous occa-
sions. Farmer, an excellent sight reader, was in constant demand for sessions ranging from jazz versions of Broadway
musicals to George Russell's experiments with the Lydian
mode. He played on *Benny Golson's New York Scene*, while
Golson supplied the tunes "Stablemates" (previously recorded
by Miles Davis) for *Portrait of Art Farmer* and "Fair Weather"
for the trumpeter's *Modern Art*, on which he also played tenor.

In 1959, Farmer and Golson formed the Jazztet, a cooperative venture similar to the one with Gryce, featuring Golson's
compositions with Farmer as the most accomplished soloist.
Golson, however, is an excellent saxophonist whose warm,
breathy style was influenced as much by Don Byas and Lucky
Thompson as by hard-bop instrumentalists. He is one of the
few modern jazz composers whose tunes—many unusual in
their structures, like "Just By Myself," whose thirty-six bars
divide into two eighteen-bar segments—have entered the repertoire as "standards." Like Gryce, Golson tended to start from
harmonies. As he told Ralph J. Gleason: "I first get an interesting chord structure laid out. I feel that this is very important
because the soloist will constantly use it for ad libbing after the
theme. I try to get a melodic line that will interweave pleas-
antly with the chord structure. When composing a ballad, I
usually create chord and melody bar by bar."[14]

Also like the Gryce–Farmer quintet, the Jazztet sought to
balance improvisation with carefully developed charts that
nonetheless would not impede swinging. But finally, like its
predecessor, it had trouble finding enough lucrative work to
hold onto a stable rhythm section and to keep the same
trombonist, since the band was a sextet. It did make some
splendid records, particularly *The Jazztet and John Lewis*,
featuring Lewis's "Bel," "Milano," "Django," "New York 19,"
"2 Degrees East, 3 Degrees West," and "Odds Against Tomorrow." Lewis, of course, was the Modern Jazz Quartet's musical
director and as remarkable a jazz composer as Golson. Another

LP, a live session entitled *The Jazztet at Birdhouse*, had a more relaxed, "jamming" feel than most Jazztet recordings and featured particularly authoritative solos by the leaders. After switching to the Mercury label, the group disbanded late in 1962.

Farmer co-led a quartet with guitarist Jim Hall for a couple of seasons, then gigged around with pianist Steve Kuhn, saxophonist and composer Jimmy Heath, and others, and in 1968 moved to Vienna. For many years he performed more frequently in Europe than in the United States. Golson also visited Europe in the mid-sixties, but in 1967 he decided to settle in Los Angeles, where he began writing for television and virtually stopped playing. Commenting in 1978 on his then recent "comeback," he told Leonard Feather: "I've been desperately trying to be sure that I didn't slide behind—at least not too far behind. Because I never did get to the avant-garde thing . . . During the time when I wasn't playing—and this might sound crazy—I was doing a lot of thinking, you know, when I'd hear things. My heart was really in it and many times I wondered when those years were going by and I didn't even take the horn out of the case, how would I do what they're doing. How would I be functioning as part of what's going on. And I'd be humming and thinking what would I be playing.

"When I came back, it was very hard. I never realized it would be so hard. It was the hardest thing I've ever done in music, to pick that horn up after eight years. It took me months just to get a sound again. The lips were like tomatoes—I had no control. It hurt my horn, for it to rest there. Just everything. It was horrible!"[15]

Gryce dropped out of jazz in 1963 and never made a comeback. He died in 1983 in Pensacola, Florida. The Jazztet, however, was revived in 1984 with its original trombonist, Curtis Fuller, and a relatively constant rhythm section featuring pianist Mickey Tucker and bassist Ray Drummond. Today, the group plays with more distinction than ever. Farmer has matured, saying even more with fewer notes, honing his sound (now on fluegelhorn) and conception to produce solos of enormous compressed power. Golson still writes tunes that stick in the mind, arresting in their melodies and original in structure. Fuller's style has also ripened. Like Farmer, he has burnt away excess and sought to purify his lines. Today, all three musicians are respected elder statesmen, performing throughout the world and looked up to by an emerging generation of young traditionalists.

Detroit Pianists

If bands like Hampton's provided one opportunity for young jazzmen to grow together, other nuclei sprang up in towns like Detroit and Philadelphia. In an interview with Whitney Balliett, Tommy Flanagan remembered the Motown scene of his youth: "There were older Detroit guys like Milt Jackson and Hank Jones and Lucky Thompson, who left early and came back to play gigs, and there were local guys like Willie Anderson, who never left . . . And there was a whole bunch of us—some younger, some older—who didn't get away so fast: Roland Hanna, who went to school with me; Paul Chambers; Doug Watkins; Donald Byrd; Kenny Burrell (he loved Oscar Moore, and we put together a Nat Cole–type trio); Sonny Red Kyner; Barry Harris; Pepper Adams, who came from Rochester and played clarinet when I first knew him; Curtis Fuller; Billy Mitchell; Yusef Lateef; Tate Houston; Frank Gant; Frank Rosolino; Parky Groat; Thad Jones and Elvin Jones, who are Hank Jones's brothers and came from Pontiac, a little way out; Art Mardigan; Oliver Jackson; Doug Mettome; Frank Foster, who's from Cincinnati; Joe Henderson; J. R. Monterose; Roy Brooks; Louis Hayes; Julius Watkins; Terry Pollard; Bess Bonnier; Alice Coltrane; and the singers Betty Carter and Sheila Jordan.

"We gave weekly concerts at a musicians' collective—the World Stage Theatre. We worked at clubs like the Blue Bird and Klein's Showbar and the Crystal and the Twenty Grand. We played in the Rouge Lounge, and at El Sino, where Charlie Parker worked. As teen-agers, we'd stand outside the screen door by the bandstand, looking in at Bird. All this lasted into the mid-fifties. Then people began to leave—Billy Mitchell ended up with Dizzy Gillespie, Thad Jones with Count Basie, Paul Chambers with Paul Quinichette, Doug Watkins with Art Blakey, Louis Hayes with Horace Silver. I stayed around until 1956, when Kenny Burrell and I left for New York."[16]

The pianists in this crowd—Hank Jones (b. 1918), Barry Harris (b. 1929), and Flanagan himself (b. 1932)—have in recent years produced one brilliant record after another, establishing themselves (along with two others, Roland Hanna and Hugh Lawson) as the most solid modern-jazz keyboard corps around. All are superb accompanists, and all have cultivated styles that offer subtle pleasures. Chronologically, the first among them was Hank Jones, the eldest member of a family that includes brother Elvin, famous for his volcanic eruptions behind John Coltrane, and the now deceased trumpeter and arranger Thad.

While Hank Jones speaks respectfully of pianists as varied as Fats Waller, Art Tatum, Bud Powell, and Al Haig, his playing derives from the Teddy Wilson and Nat Cole school of the late 1930s and early 1940s. His light, harplike touch, as though he were plucking the piano's strings instead of striking its keys, and his gracefully restrained single-note style are a reformulation of their aesthetic in modern jazz terms. A pianist of great flexibility, he can not only "fit in" with but inspire and stimulate instrumentalists ranging from Artie Shaw to Jackie McLean, as well as singers of every variety, from Andy Williams to Ella Fitzgerald.

Jones played his first New York gig and made his record debut in 1944 with trumpeter and blues singer Hot Lips Page. Since then, he has worked with so many jazz musicians that it would take pages to list them all. Some of his more notable associations were with Fitzgerald (1948–1953), Benny Goodman, Coleman Hawkins, Charlie Parker, and Lester Young. In addition, he was virtually Savoy Records' "house pianist" in the middle and late 1950s, though this didn't keep him from recording for at least a dozen other labels during the same period. His exquisite sensitivity, and the refinement of his musical thinking, placed him high on everyone's list of favorite pianists.

This refinement can be heard in Jones's solos on tunes like "Autumn Leaves" (from Cannonball Adderley's *Somethin' Else*, Blue Note) and "One for My Baby" (from Wes Montgomery's *So Much Guitar*, Riverside). Here—and on scores of other LPs—Jones achieves one of the most deeply relaxed grooves in jazz history. He provides a model of alert yet unintrusive accompaniment, while his solos combine ascending and descending runs of carefully modulated dynamics, deft funky touches, and a flexible rhythmic sense that constantly pushes and pulls at the beat. Jones also recorded under his own name in the late 1950s, perhaps most successfully on a solo album for Savoy and on another LP entitled simply *The Trio* (with bassist Wendell Marshall and Kenny Clarke) for the same label. This latter disc is one of jazz's secret after-hours classics. Marshall's velvety bass and Clarke's perfect wrist control on brushes lay down a cushion of sound as they mesh with Jones's dancing, skipping lines on medium tempos and his lushly strummed chords and bell-like octaves on ballads.

For a while, Jones's very discretion and "good taste," along with his fifteen years buried in the CBS staff orchestra, seemed to condemn him to an obscurity similar to but worse than Wynton Kelly's, since Kelly at least performed regularly in jazz clubs. During the last fifteen years, however, he has been rediscovered by a new generation of listeners (in 1979 alone he recorded at least six albums under his own name). Jones is now, like Farmer and Golson, in demand around the world and esteemed as an elder statesman of modern jazz.

One fellow Detroiter Jones influenced was Tommy Flanagan. The two have recorded a duet album (*Our Delights* on Galaxy), and many of the same adjectives have been applied to their playing: "gentle" and "delicate," for example. Reminisc-

ing to Michael Ullman about his native city's profusion of
keyboard artists, Flanagan commented: "There was a lot of
playing in Detroit—a lot of pianos. It didn't matter what part of
town. If anybody in the house played an instrument, they also
had a piano. There was always a place to have a session,
whether it was my house or not. We used to play with Kenny
[Burrell], or at Barry Harris's."[17] Like Jones, Flanagan admires
Nat Cole and Teddy Wilson; he has referred to Jones as "a more
modern Wilson."[18] Also like Jones, he has worked as Ella
Fitzgerald's accompanist, first from 1963 to 1965 and again for
a ten-year stint that began in 1968.

It was Flanagan's move to New York City in 1956 (along
with guitarist Burrell, who has called him his "running
buddy . . . we're the same age. We started out together—had
our first gig together"[19]) that signaled the beginning of his
recording career. Over the next few years, he appeared as a
sideman on dates led by Burrell, John Coltrane (*Giant Steps*,
one of Trane's most intriguing discs, an experiment with ultra-
dense, thick and fast chord changes), Miles Davis, Coleman
Hawkins, J.J. Johnson, and Sonny Rollins. During a European
tour with Johnson in 1957, Flanagan cut his first album as a
leader: *The Tommy Flanagan Trio Overseas*, with bassist
Wilbur Little and Elvin Jones.

The record contains at least one example of Flanagan's silky,
caressing approach to ballads: "Chelsea Bridge," the beginning
of a long love affair on wax with Billy Strayhorn tunes. But in
general it is a rocking, kicking session booted along by Jones's
busily interweaving, loose-jointed brushwork. Flanagan has
always played longer, twistier melodic lines than Hank Jones,
and his prickly, vigorous attack is more percussive. Though
not every cut is a blues, the whole side has a bluesy feel and
includes two walking, medium-tempo blues: "Skal Brothers"
and "Little Rock." "Skal Brothers" relies on a call-and-
response pattern for its down-home atmosphere, while "Little
Rock" creates an intimate mood of *ad hoc* experimentation—
of trying things out in a last set or after closing time, when so

much of the best jazz gets created. The LP concludes with two
slow numbers close both to Duke Ellington's compositions
and to what used to be called "blues ballads," and Flanagan's
solo on the last of these, "Willow Weep for Me," builds to an
exultantly shouting climax.

Still another pianist with whom Flanagan has performed
duets is Barry Harris. In fact, one of the most dramatic jazz
performances I ever witnessed was the two of them playing
beneath the stone arches at Manhattan's 79th Street boat basin
while a storm approached from New Jersey and jagged lightning bolts rent the heavens. They had met early on in Detroit,
shared an instructor (Gladys Dillard, whom Flanagan recalls as
teaching "the correct pianistic attack—how to finger correctly
and use the tips of my fingers"[20]), and often practiced
together—along with other young musicians like Pepper
Adams and Paul Chambers—at Harris's house. Despite *The
Tommy Flanagan Trio Overseas* and other evidence to the
contrary, Flanagan has always been considered a lyricist.
Harris, on the other hand, though he also has a way with
ballads, is known as a driving, smoking instrumentalist. He
first ventured out of Detroit in 1956, replacing Richie Powell—
who had perished in the same automobile accident that killed
Clifford Brown—in Max Roach's quintet. Harris soon returned
home, however, and stayed in Detroit until 1960 when, after a
brief period with Cannonball Adderley, he settled in New York
City. Like Jones and Flanagan, Harris has performed with
Swing musicians—in particular, Coleman Hawkins—but he is
more of a dyed-in-the-wool modernist than his two Motor City
compatriots. Whereas Jones and Flanagan, even at their blues-
iest, radiate sunshine and civility, Harris partakes somewhat
of hard bop's darker energies, especially on medium-tempo
tunes, where he can establish deeply hypnotic grooves.

Harris has made his mark especially as a keeper of the bebop
flame. In an interview with Bob Rusch, he bristled at the very
term "hard bop": "I don't even know what you mean when
you're talking about hard bop—bop is bop as far as I'm con-

cerned. And when you think of bop and that's Bird and Diz—
we don't have too much bop ever—I'm a purist."[21] In recent
years, Harris has often paid tribute, on records and in person, to
Tadd Dameron, Thelonious Monk, and Bud Powell and has
expressed his skepticism about the value of changes in jazz
since the 1940s.

A disc like *Barry Harris at the Jazz Workshop* (recorded in
1960 with Sam Jones and Louis Hayes, Harris's teammates in
Cannonball's rhythm section) certainly pays its respects to
bebop, most obviously in tunes by or associated with Charlie
Parker and Dizzy Gillespie ("Moose the Mooche," "Star Eyes,"
"Don't Blame Me," and "Woody'n You"). Yet the only track
with a genuinely "boppish" air is Harris's own "Curtain Call,"
a bright fanfare that leads into a fleet piano solo in the style of
Bud Powell, though without the quicksilvery surprise and
sense of discovery that we find in Bud's best work. The other
cuts, except for "Don't Blame Me," which also owes something to Bud's somber readings of ballads like "Embraceable
You," are medium tempo. Harris's touch is weighty, deliberate. He embeds himself in the beat instead of skimming over it
or floating upon it as beboppers often had, and this—together
with Jones's solidity and Hayes's fiercely purposeful drumming—creates a heavy swing that is one of the record's strong
points. Harris often comes down hard on the first beats of
phrases that then seem to trail away (in Whitney Balliett's
words) "as if they were being blown out of hearing."[22] All these
factors make for an emphasis on "cooking." More than Hank
Jones or Tommy Flanagan, Harris is a pianist you pop your
fingers to.

But the three do have much in common. All are "musicians'
musicians"—that is, masters of nuance who appeal to edu-
cated tastes, to listeners who can get beneath the surface of
jazz, its overall "sound," and savor the dynamics and imagina-
tive eccentricities of specific solos. As Gary Giddins noted: "In
the 1980s, they practically monopolize classical bop piano."[23]
Yet ironically, they are more conservative than the inventors

of classical bop piano. In a sense, artists like Jones, Flanagan, and Harris, as well as Farmer and Golson, may represent what modern jazz would have been had the bebop revolution not taken place under the sign of radical innovation. Without Bird, Monk, et al., jazz would certainly have evolved since the 1940s, but perhaps in a less flamboyant and iconoclastic manner. This relatively subdued manner—along with the emphasis on "beauty" that led Blue Note to reject Harris—is the source of these lyrical stylists' affinities with the great Swing musicians. Like Benny Carter, Duke Ellington, and so many others associated with Swing, they have improved over the years, adding layer upon layer of finish, polishing and refining their art's sheen and subtle symmetry.

6

TENORS AND ORGANS

Benny Carter and Duke Ellington represent refinement and urbanity—but big-band Swing had a rawer, more "down-home" side as well. While this earthier variant is best known to jazz aficionados through the work of Count Basie's orchestra, it can be heard in many other southern and southwestern "territory bands" of the 1930s. Such bands, which included Walter Page and His Blue Devils and Milt Larkins's and Jay McShann's ensembles, performed in the main for black audiences. Mostly, they played the blues and showcased "blues shouters," like Jimmy Rushing in Basie's band, who could generate big enough sounds to be heard over seventeen wailing musicians.

Written arrangements were usually rudimentary or nonexistent. Riff-based tunes would be worked out in rehearsal and performance, "by head." Talking about his years with Basie, trumpeter Harry "Sweets" Edison remembered that "when I first joined the band we had maybe six arrangements in the entire book. Now since I was going to make music my career, I wanted to read music and learn more about it. But they kept playing and playing until I didn't know where I was. Finally I said, 'Hey, Basie, where's the music?' and he answered, 'What's the matter? You're *playing*, aren't you?' So I said, 'Yes, but I want to know *what* I'm playing.' And I said, 'When the band ends I don't know what note to hit.' Then Basie told me, 'If you hit a note tonight and it sounds right, just play that same note tomorrow.' "[1]

This Texas-Oklahoma-Kansas City–based, riff-oriented, hard-and-sinewy orchestral sound was to have a long life in both jazz and black pop music. The backgrounds for most of B. B. King's records from the 1950s, for instance, come straight out of it. When vibraphonist Lionel Hampton left Benny Goodman and formed his first big band in 1941, he plugged into the Southwest scene. This was partly due to his friendship with guitarist Charlie Christian, who was at once a pioneer of modern jazz and a quintessential Oklahoma bluesman. Hampton also raided the Southwest for two tenors: Illinois Jacquet and Arnett Cobb, both veterans of Milt Larkins's Houston-based outfit. Jacquet, born in Louisiana and raised in Texas, scored a smash hit for Hampton with his solo on "Flying Home" in 1942. Though deep-funk tenor playing should perhaps be traced back to Ben Webster's lusty, swaggering solos, the honkin'-and-screamin' movement is usually linked to Jacquet's outing on "Flying Home" and to his antics at Jazz at the Philharmonic concerts in the mid-forties.

In their heyday, the honkers and screamers aimed at creating maximum excitement. Romping and stomping, rolling on the floor, bellowing single notes over and over, they induced paroxysms, hysteria, catharsis. Record producer Teddy Reig recalls that "when Hampton played theaters he would give everybody a fit, because he'd get into a groove and the people would be going crazy and he just wouldn't quit. He'd screw up the schedule and make overtime, and they'd have to close the curtain. And sometimes when they did that he'd take the band out in the audience. Lionel was the big band version of honking and screaming."[2]

Another of Reig's anecdotes describes the end of a concert featuring baritone honker Paul Williams, whose hits included "The Hucklebuck": "The place was in an uproar. People started screaming and running up on stage as I was closing the curtain. I ran out there and grabbed Paul's arm and said, 'Let's get out of here!'" As Williams's popularity grew in the late 1940s, crowds began lining up around the block for his appearances. "Every five minutes," says Reig, "the fire department would come in and I'd give them a bunch of tickets to count. But there were hundreds of tickets in my pockets they didn't know about. Then there was a shooting or something. Before it was over, Paul Williams closed down every dance hall in Baltimore. There wasn't one left he didn't close with a riot."

The honkers were known for their blatant showmanship. Williams, for example, paid a midget to walk along the bar doing the hucklebuck while the saxophonist walked beside him and customers dropped money into the bell of his horn. Such high jinks didn't sit well with jazz critics. Emerging simultaneously with bebop, the honkers marked a parting of the ways between highbrow and lowbrow black music—what Johnny Griffin meant when he said promoters "took the music out of Harlem and put it in Carnegie Hall and downtown in those joints where you've got to be quiet. The black people split and went back to Harlem, back to the rhythm and blues, so they could have a good time."[3]

In fact, however, Griffin's lively picture was oversimplified. He himself graced Joe Morris's R & B outfit with his big-toned, dirty solos on tunes like "Lowe Groovin'." After leaving Morris, he played with Lionel Hampton's orchestra before joining Art Blakey and then Thelonious Monk. Even in 1961, when he was firmly established as a jazz saxophonist, Griffin described himself as "a nervous person when I'm playing. I like to play fast. I get excited, and I have to sort of control myself, restrain myself. But when the rhythm section gets cooking, I want to explode."[4] Dizzy Gillespie's bebop big band featured James Moody's wild and woolly tenor work in the late 1940s. Today Illinois Jacquet, who supposedly started it all, remains a respected jazz tenorman (see his comments on bebop's genesis at Minton's in Chapter 1). Other honkers like Willis "Gator

Tail" Jackson, whose nickname comes from the title of his biggest R & B hit, later emerged as seductive balladeers in the boudoir-saxophone tradition of Ben Webster and others. If the honkers' glory days as stars in their own right were the late forties, the reverberations have nevertheless been felt ever since in both jazz and black popular music. For instance, much of the impact and musical density of Marvin Gaye records like *What's Going On* and *Here, My Dear* come from contributions of tenormen "Wild Bill" Moore and Ernie Watts, respectively. On the back of his *Ornette on Tenor* album (Atlantic), Ornette Coleman declared that "the tenor is a rhythm instrument, and the best statements Negroes have made, of what their soul is, have been on tenor saxophone. Now you think about it, and you'll see I'm right. The tenor's got that thing, that honk, you can get to people with it. Sometimes you can be playing that tenor and I'm telling you, the people want to jump across the rail."

Coleman was not the only one to think the tenor had a special relationship to black people's "soul." In 1950s R & B, for every one alto star (like Earl Bostic), there were a dozen tenormen. Most of the four-, eight-, and twelve-bar "breaks" on R & B vocals were tenor solos. In hard bop, too, in the fifties and sixties, good to very good tenors outnumbered altoists of equal stature. Rollins and Coltrane were the most influential saxophonists of the period. The initial generation of postwar honkers was diverse in its aspirations. Some—like Lee Allen of New Orleans, heard alongside Fats Domino, Smiley Lewis, Little Richard, and others—stayed within an R & B context. Others, like Johnny Griffin, gravitated toward "straight jazz" of a fairly uncompromising variety, although Griffin's fiery declamations still recall his roots. Others worked in an area on the border between jazz and R & B, creating a new kind of music that ended up being called "soul jazz." These included Eddie "Lockjaw" Davis, Gene Ammons, Arnett Cobb, Red Holloway, Willis "Gator Tail" Jackson, Ike Quebec, Jimmy Forrest, and—a little later—Stanley Turrentine, Houston Person, and Grover Washington. The basis for their playing lay in Swing saxophonists of the rowdier sort—for example, Webster or Chu Berry—but the new crop of soul-jazz saxophonists had also learned from both R & B and bebop. Among this crop, perhaps the most interesting was Eddie "Lockjaw" Davis.

Born in 1921, Davis (usually known as "Jaws" or "Lock") came of age in the late thirties, when Harlem's ballrooms were filled with dancers jitterbugging to the big-band sounds of Chick Webb, Jimmy Lunceford, and Lucky Millinder. "I really became a musician because my kid brother was a bouncer at the Savoy Ballroom up in Harlem," Jaws has commented. "I was just a kid then and he used to let me in for free. I used to take it all in, you know: the lights, the noise, the music. This was the big band era and the biggest guys there were the musicians. They got the awe, the girls and all the admiration. I thought straight off, that's for you man. In the big bands, the big guys were usually the drummer and the saxophone player. The drums were a bit cumbersome but I could manage a horn so I settled for the saxophone."[5]

Eight months after he first picked up an instrument, Jaws was playing in an ensemble (including Bud Powell) that was hired one night in its entirety, minus saxophonist Rudy Williams, by trumpeter Cootie Williams. Cootie Williams's orchestra, whose book included arrangements by Tadd Dameron and Thelonious Monk and whose theme song was Monk's "Epistrophy," played at Harlem's Savoy Ballroom, "the Home of Happy Feet," and then, Jaws recalls, "went on the RKO theater circuit with Ella Fitzgerald, the four Ink Spots, a dancer—Ralph Brown—and a comedian. It was a six-month tour: three months north and three months south."[6] After leaving Cootie, Lockjaw performed with Millinder and Louis Armstrong, and from 1945 to 1952 he led the house band at Minton's Playhouse.

Jaws has cited Coleman Hawkins, Herschel Evans, Lester Young, Don Byas, and Ben Webster—all major Swing tenormen—as his "real influences."[7] In particular, he emphasizes his early friendship with Webster ("I used to hang out with Ben Webster . . . people used to call me 'Little Ben'"[8]) and Byas. Nonetheless, he has often recorded with modern-jazz musicians. The year 1946 found him in a studio leading a band called "Eddie Davis and His Beboppers" that included Fats Navarro and pianist Al Haig. This is very immature Lockjaw. From a jazz point of view, his solos are badly paced. He gets hot too soon and therefore often has nowhere to go after the first few bars. Still, a number of his virtues can already be glimpsed: his percussive approach to his ax; a penchant for descending phrases and down-bent notes that trail away melismatically; and a wonderfully insinuating vocal sound that can erupt from dark, smoky mutterings into raw urgency in a single bar. One tune, "Hollerin' and Screamin'," is a kind of raving nonstop honk-fest (even Navarro catches the spirit) that starts with a raunchy shout of joy and plunges into an orgy of bellows and screams that anticipate some "free jazz" of the 1960s.

A few years later, in 1951, Jaws recorded with trombonist Bennie Green in an ensemble that included Art Blakey. By this time, he had learned to pace himself better. On "Green Junction," a loping, exultant medium-tempo strut, his playing is far more controlled, though it still bristles with swinging energy. His sound here is more nuanced, at once relaxed and ardent. "Whirl a Licks," another tune from the same date, kicks off with a duet between Jaws and Green. The cut is a fast-paced flag-waver, yet Lockjaw's solo again is well paced, using honks and screams sparingly and building to a climax. Before taking the number out, the two soloists trade phrases and finally merge in a rip-roaring simultaneous improvisation.

Throughout the 1950s, Lockjaw recorded gutbucket R & B for King Records, including such off-color vocal ditties as "Mountain Oysters." In addition, in 1955 he formed a trio with organist Shirley Scott that would stay together till the end of the decade. By now, his jazz style had mellowed still further as he evolved into a master of the ballad. On "But Beautiful," recorded with Scott in 1958, he limits himself to playing the tune, but his time is so loose, his tone so breathy and erotically charged, and his timbre and phrasing so original that he makes it entirely his own. Indeed, by 1958 Jaws had evolved into an example of everything that gives a jazzman a "voice." Never a great musical thinker, he created a combination of hot funk and tenderness that has been his trademark ever since.

In the early 1960s, Jaws formed a two-tenor combo with Johnny Griffin that helped to solidify his jazz bonafides. As Lockjaw remembered it: "At first we had some difficulty finding engagements—probably because of the image people had of me as a honking, loud rhythm and blues performer. In fact, one guy came up to me and said that he was a club owner and had had three opportunities to book us into his place but turned them down because he thought I was strictly an R & B tenor. After hearing the quintet, he said he was happy to admit he was wrong and wanted to book us on the spot."[9]

The two-tenor idea had been tried before in modern jazz, especially by Dexter Gordon and Wardell Gray and by Gene Ammons and Sonny Stitt, but never with such musically gratifying results. The contrast between Jaws's warm sound and laid-back rhythmic sense and Griffin's impetuous rapid-fire lines made the quintet more a study in contrasts than a "battle." It recorded at least half a dozen superb albums before disbanding in 1963. One highlight was the tune "Abundance" (pronounced, in appropriately sexy fashion, "A Bun Dance"). Here we find Lockjaw in top form, playing spare, carefully constructed lines and using vibrato to grab notes and rock them from side to side at moments of peak intensity. More than anything else, the unit with Griffin established Lockjaw's place in jazz circles.

If Lockjaw (along with Gene Ammons) stands out among the older generation of soul tenors, Stanley Turrentine occupies a similar position, to my mind, among the younger group. His self-evaluation ("I know I'm not a virtuoso on my instrument, but I am a stylist"[10]) could be applied to Lockjaw too. Born in

Pittsburgh in 1934, Turrentine took up the saxophone at the age of eleven, encouraged by his father, who had played the same instrument with Al Cooper's Savoy Sultans. Turrentine's first professional gig was with Lowell Fulsom's blues band. "I guess my sound started back then," he says. "I couldn't avoid the blues. That band had a blind piano player in it, name of Ray Charles." Charles was already writing songs, which Turrentine would transcribe after they finished work in the joints and barns the band played. After leaving Fulsom, Turrentine moved to Cleveland, where he gigged with Tadd Dameron before going on the road again in Earl Bostic's R & B combo. Following two years in the army (1956–1958), he joined Max Roach.

It was at this point that Turrentine began to make an impression in the jazz world. In particular, he caught the attention of Alfred Lion, who signed him to an exclusive contract with Blue Note Records that lasted until 1969. During this ten-year period, Turrentine recorded regularly as a sideman for the label on albums by Horace Parlan, Art Taylor, Jimmy Smith, Duke Jordan, Horace Silver, Duke Pearson, and Kenny Burrell. For several years in the 1960s, he co-led a combo with his wife, organist Shirley Scott (who had previously accompanied Lockjaw). "We called it the 'Chitlins Circuit.' A lot of small places, with bad sound systems, small audiences . . . We used to deadhead a lot. Twice we drove to the coast in three days, New York to L.A., eating in the car, sleeping in the car, with the organ in a little trailer in the back. You'd get there to the gig and for days you'd still feel like you're still riding. It's funny now; it wasn't so funny then. We'd get to clubs where the hallways were too narrow for the organ, and once in Virginia, we had to carry the organ up three flights of fire escapes. But for all that, we'd go in that night and we'd blow our hearts out."[11]

Turrentine's work has been remarkably consistent, and he's still going strong, as his performances on Jimmy Smith's recent *Off the Top* LP show. When he hit the scene in 1960, "soul jazz" was something of a fad. Prestige Records ran ads in *Down Beat* saying: "Despite opposition of critics, Prestige gave birth to soul jazz,"[12] while references to "soul," "funk," and black cuisine seemed to crop up in the titles of half the albums issued. Some of the "soul" being purveyed was more jive than real, but Turrentine was the genuine article. As Clifford Jordan put it: "Some people can play that and really extend that, like King Curtis or Stanley Turrentine. They can play that little snap. It's right in their body and they're not trying to imitate nobody. It's a natural feeling that they project."

Turrentine's "snap" (described by Michael James as his "pronounced taste for inflections, often bending the final note of a phrase upward in a most unusual and effective way"[13]) is pervasive on *That's Where It's At*, a side he cut for Blue Note with pianist Les McCann, bassist Herbie Lewis, and drummer Otis Finch. Except for the ballad ("Dorene Don't Cry I: . . ."), all the numbers are either blues or near-blues. What first leaps out and grabs the listener's attention is Turrentine's sweet yet muscular sound, which suggests Johnny Hodges more than the classic Swing tenors. A flexible voice, it can deepen to a resonant honk, soar into one of the most piercingly full-throated cries in jazz, and broaden to a thick, sensuous vibrato on ballads. Turrentine tends to play on top of the beat, making for a deep, trancelike groove, and his phrasing draws on both modern jazz and R & B. Angular lines alternate with timeless blues phraseology. *That's Where It's At*, which represents "soul jazz" at its most eloquent, also owed much to McCann's orchestral blues- and gospel-soaked style, as well as to the exquisite ballad he contributed to the date. (McCann has composed a number of memorable ballads, another of which, "Fayth, You're . . . ," can be heard on his *Les McCann in New York* album.)

If the tenor was one pillar of soul jazz, the other was the electric organ—to be exact the Hammond B-3—which in effect was given its jazz debut by Jimmy Smith in 1955. Although Smith legitimized the instrument in jazz, he did not, of course, invent it. As early as the 1920s, we find Fred Longshaw accompanying Bessie Smith on harmonium. Fats Waller also made some brilliant recordings on pipe organ in the late 1930s. He had started playing the instrument in his father's Abyssinian Baptist Church in Harlem and later worked as house organist at the Lincoln Theatre in the same neighborhood. The detail about Waller's church backgound is significant, for the electric organ really evolved as an important instrument in black music in the context of gospel. It also gained a certain standing among Swing musicians. Count Basie doubled on electric organ, while Milt Buckner, a veteran of Lionel Hampton's band, made it his primary instrument after 1952. But perhaps the most important piano-to-organ switch prior to Jimmy Smith's was Wild Bill Davis's—among other things because hearing him in 1953 inspired Smith to do likewise.

Davis, who had been pianist and arranger for Louis Jordan's jazz-and-blues ensemble between 1945 and 1948, pioneered a roaring, excitement-building approach to his instrument that made him a natural choice when Lockjaw Davis decided to cut a tenor-and-organ album: "One of the ventures I did at that time was a tenor and organ record. This was in 1951. I wanted to do it with Wild Bill Davis who was working as a single then, but he had a contract with another record company so I used Bill Doggett, who had been a pianist with Ella Fitzgerald. On bass we had Oscar Pettiford and the drummer was Shadow Wilson. This was the first organ and tenor album. It came out on Royal Roost Records and sold very well in the States. I made some more afterwards with Doc Bagby for King."[14]

Doggett, who had also worked with Louis Jordan, went on to record a string of hits for King. The biggest of these was "Honky Tonk," which sold four million copies and helped him win Cashbox magazine's awards as top R & B performer in 1957, 1958, and 1959. Another pioneer (this time in jazz rather than R & B) was Les Strand, whom Smith has called "the

Tatum of the organ."[15] Strand began playing bebop on his instrument in the late 1940s and recorded several albums for the Fantasy label in the fifties.

The Hammond B-3, a now endangered species no longer being manufactured, offered jazz/R & B performers a number of advantages. It produced a huge sound that could compete with the ghetto's most boisterous audiences. It was also the first synthesizer, and as such could generate a variety of tones. While these tones had little in common with the instruments they purportedly replicated—such as "trumpet"—they certainly offered a wide range of effects. The B-3's pedal could produce a bass line that enabled the organ to replace both piano and string bass. And in general, there was something raucous, something down and dirty, in its array of electronic growls, wails, moans, and shrill ostinato tidal waves that immediately appealed to black ears. Indeed, every jazz organist of note has been black, from Jimmy Smith to Larry Young and Charles Earland; and the organ's hoarse, raspy tonal quality is far closer to blues singing than the piano's is.

Smith was born in 1926 in Norristown, Pennsylvania. As a child he studied piano, and at the age of nine won a prize on *Major Bowes' Amateur Hour.* "Music was just part of my life as far back as I can remember," he has commented. "I was about sixteen when I teamed up with my father to do a song and dance routine in local night clubs. I kept on gigging around locally through the 1940s, except for the time when I was in the service."[16]

In the late forties Smith also studied string bass and piano, respectively, at Philadelphia's Hamilton and Ornstein Schools of Music. In the meantime, he played piano with groups like Bobby Edwards and His Dial-Tones and Johnny Sparrow and His Bows and Arrows around Newark and Philly, and in 1951 he joined Donald Gardner and His Sonotones, an R & B outfit. He stayed with Gardner until 1954, but after 1953 he spent his days perfecting his technique on the organ, whose possibilities he felt "hadn't been fully explored."

In 1955, having emerged from the woodshed, Smith opened in Atlantic City, leading a trio that included a guitarist and drummer. Word of his prowess and his startling approach to his ax had been spreading through the jazz grapevine, and artists flocked to hear him. One of these was singer and composer Babs Gonzales, who wrote the liner notes for Smith's first two LPs on Blue Note Records: "Last summer he opened at a club in Atlantic City. He didn't need any 'tubs' because all the drummers there were lined up nightly waiting for a chance to play with him. Within three days news reached me about this 'insane' organist and I drove down to 'dig' for myself.

"What I heard was a 'cat' playing forty choruses of 'Georgia Brown' in pure 'Nashua' tempo and never repeating. I heard 'future stratospheric' sounds that were never before explored on the organ. I was supposed to see a host of 'cats' that night, but all I did was 'lay dead' because every cat in town made it by Jimmy's 'gig' during the night."

A few months later, Smith was rocking the house in New York City spots like Small's Paradise in Harlem and Café Bohemia in Greenwich Village. Partly at Gonzales's urging, Blue Note owners Alfred Lion and Frank Woolf journeyed to Smalls's to hear the new star. Woolf has left us a vivid description of his first encounter with Smith: "It was at Smalls in January of 1956. He was a stunning sight. A man in convulsions, face contorted, crouched over in apparent agony, his fingers flying, his foot dancing over the pedals. The air was filled with waves of sound I had never heard before. A few people sat around, puzzled but impressed. Jimmy came off the stand, smiling . . . 'So what do you think?' he asked. 'Yeah!' I said. That's all I could say. Alfred Lion had already made up his mind.

"Right from the inception of his recording career, he was in full command of this very complex and demanding machine. Apart from his incredible technique he had fire, feeling, beat, humor—all adding up to a highly personal style. Everything was there, everything was right, when he did 'The Champ' and on through all the other masterpieces in the years that followed."[17]

"The Champ" was the eight-minute showpiece on Smith's second Blue Note LP. What we hear, on this and his other early recordings, is an intoxicated delight in the organ's many voices, its huge sound and textural variety. In addition, we discover a master of blues vocabulary who is also familiar with bebop and ready to use the two styles contrapuntally. From the first, with singles like "The Champ" and Horace Silver's "The Preacher," Smith hit big on ghetto jukeboxes, where the ground had been prepared by Wild Bill Davis and Bill Doggett. Yet at the same time, he was being compared by Leonard Feather and others to Bud Powell for his dazzling technique and to electric guitarist Charlie Christian and bassist Jimmy Blanton, both of whom established their instruments as major jazz solo vehicles in the early 1940s. In the 1957 *Metronome Year Book*, Smith was declared 1956's New Star.

Over the next few years, Smith recorded dozens of times for Blue Note, often with his trio but also in larger hard-bop ensembles that included trumpeters Blue Mitchell, Donald Byrd, and Lee Morgan and saxophonists Hank Mobley, Lou Donaldson, Jackie McLean, Tina Brooks, and Ike Quebec. During this period, Smith's style matured. His exuberance and "look ma, no hands!" attitude, his joy in the organ's multifarious possibilities and his wish to try them all out at once were brought under control. As the English critic Jack Cooke noted in 1961: "It seems perfectly obvious now, though it was less so at the time, that what must take place within Smith's style was a process of refinement, of shedding rather than adding; an intelligible idiom, based on the fundamental laws and principles of the electric organ, out of the mass of occasionally unrelated accomplishments which he possessed and was using with such liberality.

"A study of the recordings Smith has made since 1956 will indicate how this painstaking process of refinement took

place; exuberance curbed and a considerable amount of discipline and forethought introduced into his playing."¹⁸

As these words were written, Smith was enjoying enormous
success on a series of records (the first was *Midnight Special,*
recorded in 1960) that featured Stanley Turrentine and either
Kenny Burrell or Quentin Warren on guitar. Still another
outstanding side from the same period, at least as good as the
ones with Turrentine but not quite so successful commercially, was *Home Cookin'* with Burrell, saxophonist Percy
France, and drummer Donald Bailey. All the tunes on it are
blues or blues based, yet each is different from the others. They
range from a very slow, after-hours groove on "See See Rider"
to a briskly rocking, head-shaking, blues-shouting version of
Ray Charles's "I Got a Woman." The record shows off many
aspects of Smith's technique, including his solid bass lines and
what Gonzales called "the only 'Oklahoma funkish' style of
comping on the Blues since Charlie Christian."¹⁹ Smith's
solos benefit greatly from his two-handed approach, his attention to dynamics, his structural sense, and, of course, his
phenomenal swing. Phrases that arch upward and then tumble
back upon themselves alternate with chords, figures played
against screaming held notes, and basic blues licks. Interweaving in classic call-and-response style, Burrell and Smith get
into some genuine duets. Today *Home Cookin'* remains one of
the great jazz-and-blues dates. Another, also featuring the
same duo, is *Blue Bash* on the Verve label. For sheer élan and
down-home funk, they have rarely been equaled.

In the late fifties and early sixties, a number of other
musicians—mostly pianists—followed Smith's lead in taking
up the electric organ. Among them were Shirley Scott, whom
we have encountered with both Lockjaw Davis and Stanley
Turrentine, and Richard "Groove" Holmes, so renowned for
his bass-line footwork that other organists would come to
watch him and try to learn his secrets. Still another was Jack
McDuff, who in the early sixties led a quartet with tenor

saxophonist Red Holloway, guitarist George Benson, and drummer Joe Dukes that could get into one of the meanest, most absorbing grooves ever heard or—alternatively—generate enough heat to lift the roof off any club or dance hall. Before striking out on his own, McDuff had backed up "Gator Tail" Jackson; and in fact, by the early sixties, boss tenors and R & B–tinged organists had come to seem a natural combination. The music they created was unpretentious. As McDuff put it: "We play that good-time thing. We play the way we feel . . . It's always been a happy thing; play and swing and have a good time. No formula."[20] In interviews and liner notes, soul-jazz artists often sounded defensive about the fact that they weren't pushing back the boundaries of Afro-American music but rather playing to what Joe Fields of Muse Records called a "jazz-oriented, finger-snappin', ass-shakin' black population." Yet much of what they created has stood the passage of time very well. Few young jazz experimentalists of the 1960s could caress a ballad with the depth and authority of Jackson playing "My One and Only Love" or Houston Person giving us "The Nearness of You." Among the youngsters who could do so, Archie Shepp acknowledged his debt to Lockjaw both in so many words and with every breathy phrase he blew, while Joe Henderson had worked the "chitlin' circuit" (clubs in the black neighborhoods of cities like Cleveland, Newark, and Pittsburgh) with Jack McDuff.

Jazz as "high art" has always drawn sustenance from jazz as "folk art." Often it's not clear which is "better." The classic comparison is between Duke Ellington and Count Basie, who was less "highbrow" yet equally sublime in his way. Indeed, it is one of jazz's problems today that there's not much of a "chitlin' circuit" left to come up through. Thus it's harder for young musicians to acquire a grounding in the basics of rhythm, voice, and delivery—that is, to draw nourishment from the wellsprings of black North American song. Anyone who has heard McDuff, or Person, tear up a neighborhood joint before an audience of his peers, all drinking, carrying on, hustling, trying to make out yet deeply attuned to the sounds being laid down, has drunk from these same wellsprings.

As soul jazz of the tenor-and-organ sort came to sound stale in the 1970s, some performers (like George Benson or, to a lesser degree, Stanley Turrentine) moved into pop music and began to make big money. Others, like "Gator Tail" Jackson, went on playing a steadily contracting black club circuit. Still others, like Groove Holmes, virtually dropped out of sight, at least as far as records are concerned. Only one—and this from the early sixties on—had moved into a more adventuresome sort of jazz: Larry Young, whom McDuff has called "the Trane of the organ."[21] After a soul-jazz apprenticeship, Young began adapting McCoy Tyner's ideas to the organ and made a couple of brilliant, ground-breaking records for Blue Note: *Into Somethin'* and *Unity*. Then he seemed to lose his bearings, veering off into a particularly muddy version of "free jazz" and later into fusion. Unfortunately, he died before he could reorient himself, and no one has followed up on his ideas. Today soul jazz survives more than thrives, yet its best living practitioners—including Jimmy Smith, Jack McDuff, Houston Person, and Stanley Turrentine—can still swing up a storm in person and on records, where they are heard mainly thanks to Joe Fields and to Person himself, who has produced many dates for the Muse label. Not only musical basics but also emotional ones can be found in their work: the joy, tenderness, and pain of existence, and the hard battle to wrench transcendence out of daunting circumstances.

7

THE POWER OF BADNESS

Soul jazz's purpose, in Stanley Turrentine's words, was "to help people relax and enjoy,"[1] but hard bop often expressed and provoked more troubling emotions. In this sense, perhaps the first authentic hard bopper was Billie Holiday. True, some of her earlier recordings—for instance, "Miss Brown to You" or "What a Little Moonlight Can Do"—possess a kind of jaunty insouciance, yet even these are shadowed by a defiant irony that cuts against their gaiety. Irony, despair, and rage are what we mostly find in her later work, as her voice rotted away, her troubles multiplied, and she fell deeper and deeper into the toils of heroin addiction and alcoholism. But the defiance remained, along with a will to triumph through the artistic act itself, creating the kind of spectral, self-lacerating beauty we hear in songs like "You're My Thrill" and "Don't Explain."

Holiday described "Ain't Nobody's Business If I Do," another tune she was extremely fond of, as "more than a song to me. It spells the way of life I tried to live, personal freedom, to hell with what-will-people-think-people, and all that":[2]

> If I go to church on Sunday
> then cabaret all day Monday,
> ain't nobody's business if I do.

117

I swear I won't call no copper
if I'm beat up by my papa.
Ain't nobody's business if I do.

Now that's a "bad" song, to be sure, by the normal definition, but what exactly is badness in black music? What did
James Brown mean when he proclaimed that he was "su-
perbad"? At times "badness" can refer to musical qualities:
heightened alertness to timbral and rhythmic values, and the
blues-inflected melodic vocabulary that makes a musician's
solo style "funky." Thus it is that jazzmen of essentially sunny
dispositions, like Cannonball Adderley or Wynton Kelly, are
sometimes described as "bad." But in general, and certainly in
order to claim "superbadness," one must also project an atmosphere of menace. In black pop music, James Brown epitomized this quality, and it is partly for this reason that rappers
today acknowledge him as their most important precursor, for
whatever its other virtues and defects, rap is certainly the
"baddest" music currently being produced in the USA.

In jazz, Lee Morgan in the late 1950s and early 1960s was just
about the baddest thing going. His statement, "I'm an extrovert person . . . and hard bop is played by bands of extrovert
people,"[3] is more a smokescreen than an insight and does
nothing to explain how he differs from more congenial extro-
verts like Adderley. What Lee possessed and Cannonball
lacked, at least by comparison, was *malice*. On "Caribbean
Fire Dance" on Joe Henderson's *Mode for Joe* album, the
trumpeter manages to make his colleagues—Henderson,
trombonist Curtis Fuller, vibist Bobby Hutcherson, pianist
Cedar Walton, bassist Ron Carter, and drummer Joe Chambers, all pretty "bad cats" themselves—sound like a bunch of
sissies beside him. The tune itself is "mean," consisting of a
tension-building minor vamp underlined by an obsessively
repeated cross-rhythmic piano figure and an explosive release
that together create an air of foreboding. Lee's solo opens with
a raw, guttural cry that cuts through all this polymetric layer-

ing like a knife. The cry is repeated and then gives way to an urgently tumbling figure, also repeated, that falls behind the beat as it comes to a close. The total effect thus created is one of urgency held under iron control. The rest of Morgan's solo is marked by constant rhythmic displacements in counterpoint to the piano, bass, and drums, by blues-based phraseology, by his typically sardonic tone, and by key notes almost always bent, slurred, or half-valved: all elements in one of the most searingly dramatic trumpet styles in modern jazz.

Mode for Joe, like almost all Morgan's records under his own leadership, appeared on the Blue Note label. Alfred Lion and Frank Woolf, the owners, consistently sought out and recorded the baddest hard boppers in New York. Refugees from Nazi Berlin who arrived in the United States shortly before the outbreak of the Second World War, they explained their purposes in their first catalogue, published in 1939: "Hot jazz, therefore, is expression and communication, a musical and social manifestation, and Blue Note records are concerned with identifying its impulse, not its sensational and commercial adornments."

During the next thirty years, Blue Note recorded Fats Navarro, Milt Jackson, Tadd Dameron, Bud Powell, J.J. Johnson, Thelonious Monk, Miles Davis, Sonny Rollins, Jackie McLean, Horace Silver, Art Blakey, Andrew Hill, and many others—more than five hundred sides altogether. Many sessions, moreover, never reached the record store bins because they lacked the polish Lion and Woolf demanded. The opportunities Blue Note gave to young and unknown artists, and its policy of paying for rehearsal time, made it unusual among independent jazz labels. The album covers were also unusual, striking in their austere, high-modernist beauty. These were the work of prize-winning designer Reid Miles and producer-photographer Woolf, a portraitist highly attuned to the musicians' fleeting moods and possessed of a subtle compositional sense.

All these factors, plus the distinctive "Blue Note sound"

achieved by engineer Rudy van Gelder, contributed to the label's mystique in the fifties and sixties: a mystique comparable to that enjoyed by New Directions Books in avant-garde literary circles. I myself remember, as a teenager, sometimes buying Blue Note discs without even knowing who the artists were, so complete was my faith in Lion's and Woolf's perspicacity. In addition, the two producers' taste for hard bop at its most uncompromising was rare among whites in the music business. As Bobby Hutcherson put it: "Alfred and Frank were more like jazz musicians than record executives. They loved to hang out and have a great time."[4] This amalgam of a severe aesthetic akin to Bauhaus perspectives and an informed passion for Afro-American music was extraordinarily productive. More than any other record company in the history of jazz, Blue Note actually affected the evolution of the music.

If, in record producer Bob Porter's words, "the difference between Blue Note and Prestige was two days' rehearsal,"[5] this was nowhere more evident than in the case of Jackie McLean, who switched from Prestige to Blue Note in 1959. Jackie could play as aggressively as Lee Morgan. But he also possessed a poignant—even tragic—sensibility that brought him close to Billie Holiday, whom he remembers as an important personal influence: "Yeah, it is true, very true [that his approach owed something to Holiday's] . . . there was something in her emotion and expression, the way she approached the melody, the way she didn't just sing a melody straight, the way she bent notes and stuff, the feeling that comes with her sound: that was something that I wanted to have."

Jackie's dates for Prestige had their moments—in particular, two somber ballads by Mal Waldron: "Abstraction" and "Mirage," which appeared, respectively, on *4,5, and 6* and *Jackie McLean & Co.* But those sessions did generally suffer from lack of preparation. McLean's angry comments on the company, quoted by A. B. Spellman, could be applied to many small jazz labels of the period: "If you can imagine being under the Nazi regime and not knowing it, then you've got an idea of what it's like to be with that company. I was starving when I signed that contract. The baby was being born, so I was glad to get my name on a record and make some money. And my condition didn't help either; any money was money then. Everybody made that move—Miles was with that company, Sonny Rollins, John Coltrane, and Monk. They all got out of its as soon as they could, just as I did.

"It's a perfect example of giving everything and getting nothing back. They give you a little bit of front money, and then they tell you about the royalties you are going to get after the record is released. I did a million dates for them, and all it amounted to is that I paid for the whole thing: engineer, the notes on the back of the album, the color photograph, the whole thing, out of my money. I still get statements saying that I owe that company ridiculous sums like $50,000; I'm exaggerating, but it's not much less ridiculous than that."[6]

McLean's signing with Blue Note coincided with the beginning of his four-year (1959–1963) stint with the Living Theatre. This was a particularly lucky break, since his lack of a cabaret card—a result of drug arrests—made it impossible for him to perform legally in New York City jazz clubs. As we have seen, McLean's first spurt of development occurred in the late 1940s. But when he made his debut on records with Miles Davis in 1951, the only element of his style really in place was his tone. This tone, at once hard and plaintive, along with what critic Michael James has called his "fierce enunciation" and "trenchant attack"[7] were what got him through the next eight years. In those years he barely practiced: "I never had my horn. It was always in the pawnshop from 1950 on." Even so, McLean's style slowly evolved toward greater structural coherency. Stints with Art Blakey and Charles Mingus probably helped, though in quite different ways.

Blakey urged Jackie to discipline his solos, building to logical and emotionally satisfying resolutions: "He'd say once you reach a climax it's better to back off than push and pursue."[8] Mingus, for his part, forced the young altoist to look beyond bebop orthodoxy: "I hadn't been content with what I was doing with changes yet, and here came Mingus telling me, 'Forget changes and forget about what key you're in,' and 'all notes are right' and things like that, and it kind of threw me. I was going through a hip phase then, but I find that I really got involved with Mingus and all of his things on a lot of nights. Mingus gave me my wings, more or less; Mingus made me feel like I could go out and explore because he was doing it and was accepted by the audience and loved for it."[9]

As a composer, McLean had created some striking melodies early on. Three of his compositions—"Dig," also known as "Donna"; "Dr. Jackle"; and "Minor March," later retitled "Minor Apprehension"—were all first recorded by Miles Davis and had entered the jazz repertoire as semi-standards by 1960. In that same year, for the first time, Jackie tried his hand at orchestrating for a three-horn front line consisting of himself, trumpeter Blue Mitchell, and tenor saxophonist Tina Brooks and backed by Kenny Drew, Paul Chambers, and Art Taylor. Largely self-taught as an arranger, he explained that "this was a challenge for me, because I didn't have much musical education and most of what I know about writing I found out myself."[10] The results, some of which appear on one side of the Blue Note LP *Jackie's Bag*, show his increasing maturity as a soloist and composer, as well as the benefits of Blue Note's policy of subsidizing rehearsal time.

One of these tunes, "Appointment in Ghana," opens with an almost dirgelike out-of-tempo figure by the front line. This figure then leads into a driving modal theme kicked along by Taylor's forceful accentuations and topped by the sound of Mitchell's tart trumpet. The song's harmonic basis is akin to Miles Davis's then recent modal experiments, but the melody's A-A-B-A pattern adds variety to the solos, with the B section serving as a foil to the terser A theme. McLean's statement comes first and shows his increasing rhythmic fluidity. He plays across the beat rather than on top of it, thus avoiding the stiffness that had sometimes plagued him before.

Alert to the song's textural possibilities, he exploits them by contrasting longer, more intricate phrases with short, staccato outbursts. In general, his playing is more thoughtful and melodic than it had been, though his characteristic urgency is still present. The other McLean composition, "Ballad for Doll," on which only the piano solos, is a full-bloodedly romantic tribute to his wife that shows a surprising richness of orchestration. After stating the theme, the horns breathe softly in unison behind the beginning of Drew's solo, a mixture of passion and delicacy that is a glowing extension of the composition.

Listening to "Appointment in Ghana" and "Ballad for Doll," one might have thought McLean would evolve in the direction of such polished jazzmen as Benny Golson and Art Farmer, but other records and performances in the early 1960s revealed a much more unsettled musical personality. On "Us," for instance, recorded live with Kenny Dorham, Walter Bishop, Jr., bassist Leroy Vinnegar, and Art Taylor, McLean explodes into one of his most scaldingly emotional solos. Over Taylor's driving beat, he mixes growls, penetrating cries, and edgily throaty outbursts with flatter, Coltrane-like inflections. Melodically, the solo is chaotic. At times McLean's ideas flow smoothly, but at others they seem both banal and disconnected. Yet somehow this heightens the emotional pitch, as though he had so much to *express* and tried to convert raw feeling so directly into music that he didn't have time to think. For savage intensity, the solo matches Morgan's on "Caribbean Fire Dance" and is another example of hard bop at its most relentless. In its restless straining against the limits of what his style could encompass, it also points ahead to McLean's experimental outings in the mid-1960s.

McLean and Morgan were outgoing types. (McLean still is, and this has helped him build a career as a an educator.) Both enjoyed considerable success—at least for jazzmen. Their work was respected by other musicians and admired by aficionados. (There was even a Jackie McLean Fan Club in the early 1960s. The club's credo affirmed that "we believe Jackie McLean is the most stimulating alto saxophonist on the jazz scene today. We like his style, we adore his sound, and we love his approach.") For the blistering hard bop they played, each was considered tops on his instrument. Many of the school's more uncompromising exponents, however, led a far more shadowy existence, as we have seen in the case of Elmo Hope. Another figure of this sort was tenor saxophonist Tina Brooks (1932–1974), who appeared on *Jackie's Bag* and for a while was McLean's understudy in Jack Gelber's play *The Connection*. Brooks recorded four albums as a leader for Blue Note between 1958 and 1961, but only one (*True Blue*) was issued in his lifetime. In 1985, all four were at last made available in the United States by Mosaic Records on *The Complete Blue Note Recordings of the Tina Brooks Quintets*. Though the recordings feature many of hard bop's foremost representatives, the dominant presence is Brooks. His tenor playing, at once melancholy and muscular, and the brooding quality of his compositions, determine the overall mood.

Tina (pronounced Teena, a reference to his size as a child) was born in Fayetteville, North Carolina. His father, David, played the piano and encouraged his eight children to study music. Of these, two became professionals: David, Jr. ("Bubba"), who went on to perform with Bill Doggett's combo, and Tina. In 1944 the Brooks family moved to New York City, but Tina, who kept getting beaten up by street gangs in their new neighborhood, was sent back to Fayetteville for most of his high-school education, only returning to the metropolis for his senior year. By 1950, Bubba was established as an R & B player, and Tina replaced him for parts of that year and the next in Sonny Thompson's band, making his recording debut with them for King Records. Other R & B gigs followed with Charles Brown, Joe Morris, and Amos Milburn, and in spring and summer of 1955, Tina also toured with Lionel Hampton's orchestra.

In 1956, Tina met the bebop trumpeter and composer Little

Benny Harris at the Blue Morocco, a Bronx jazz club. Harris schooled him in modern jazz's complex and demanding structures. At the same time, Tina struck up a friendship with Elmo Hope, whose dark-hued, minor tunes may have influenced his style as a composer. With these two mentors, saxophonist Jimmy Lyons, and Oliver Beener (a trumpeter who became his closest friend), Tina gigged around the Bronx and jammed wherever he could. Another member of this group, saxophonist Herman Riley, recently recalled their activities: "We'd warm up every Monday at Connie's, then go directly across the street to Small's Paradise for their famous Monday night jam sessions . . . I lived near Tina. We'd all practice during the day in the Bronx and then find a place to play at night somewhere. We'd go anywhere just to get the opportunity to play. We'd even drive to New Jersey or as far as Philadelphia. We were all just learning then and very eager."[11]

In late 1957, Benny Harris introduced Alfred Lion of Blue Note Records to Tina's playing. Favorably impressed, Lion used Tina on three Jimmy Smith sessions (issued as *Houseparty, The Sermon, Confirmation,* and *Cool Blues*) and two led by Kenny Burrell (*Blue Lights* and *On View at the Five Spot Café*). In addition, Brooks cut a record of his own with Lee Morgan (volume one of the Mosaic set).

Through Lion, Tina also met tenor saxophonist Ike Quebec, who brought him and Freddie Hubbard together. Freddie used Tina on his first Blue Note record date (*Open Sesame,* recorded June 19, 1960). A week later, Tina cut another album, *True Blue* (volume two on Mosaic). Other sessions followed, with Jackie McLean (*Jackie's Bag*), Freddie Redd (*Shades of Redd*), and Howard McGhee (*The Connection* for Felsted Records, Brooks's only recording not on Blue Note), plus another two unreleased dates under his own name (volumes three and four on Mosaic). By 1962, Brooks's career as a recording artist was over. Nonetheless, he continued to appear at Bronx jazz spots like the Blue Morocco, Freddie's Bar, and the 845 Club with Hope, Beener, and others. Heroin addiction—complete with spells in jail and in hospitals—limited his professional activity during the rest of his life. The official cause of his death in 1974 was kidney failure. He had been too ill to play for several years. As with dozens of other jazz musicians, the word "underrated" is unavoidable in connection with Tina Brooks. Even during his period of greatest visibility (1958–1961), Brooks was unnoticed by most jazz fans; and were it not for Mosaic coproducer Michael Cuscuna's belief in his work, he would be even less recognized today. Drug addiction is certainly part of the story. So, apparently, was Tina's personality. He is remembered as a self-effacing man who shied away from the kind of sociable "hanging out" that gets jazz musicians gigs. Tina's survival instincts seem to have been feebler than those of others—including some fellow junkies. As McLean put it: "Tina Brooks was a sensitive human being and a brilliant saxophonist, who was crushed under the pressures of this industry. And he took the same route that a lot of guys did: self-destruction."[12]

The four records issued by Mosaic provide our first chance to study Tina's work as a leader. Among them, volume one is the least stamped by his personality. Robert Palmer, in a perceptive essay that accompanies the set, describes it as a possible case of "too much, too soon." Certainly recording with Lee Morgan, Sonny Clark, Doug Watkins, and Art Blakey—among the sharpest-edged musicians around New York and all more battle hardened than Tina—would have intimidated most young jazzmen. The ensembles are ragged, which may account for Alfred Lion's decision not to release the date. (Lion was a stickler for tight, precise heads, and this was undoubtedly one of the reasons for his rehearsal policy.) Nonetheless, most of the key elements of Tina's style are already in place: a plaintive, sinewy tone; a floating, legato rhythmic sense not unlike Lester Young's; and an ability, similar to McLean's at the time, to compensate through timbre and "presence" for sometimes commonplace melodic ideas. Blakey is his usual volcanic self, Watkins is rock solid, and Clark shows his penchant for intricate, snakingly long-lined solos. This record also, like several others of the period, catches Lee Morgan in transition between Clifford Brown's effervescence and the more aggressive style he later cultivated. Of the tunes, only one, in retrospect, can be deemed a true Tina Brooks composition: "Minor Move," which, despite its title, has a lushly chorded major bridge.

The "Spanish" or "Latin" tinges we find in "Minor Move" are pervasive in Tina's later compositions, where they usually mean minor melodies and emphatic rhythmic patterning. Frequently, they are balanced by strikingly "pretty" major changes on the bridge. On *True Blue,* Tina's next date as a leader, such tunes—"Good Old Soul," "Theme for Doris," and (a variant: pretty tune with Latin vamp) "Miss Hazel"—predominate. As a soloist, Tina also sounds bolder and more sharply defined. Drawing on his R & B background, he uses slurred notes, honks, and other vocal inflections in counterpoint to a supple rhythmic sense that makes his solos seem to soar above the rhythm section. The combination, enriched by his mournful tone, works especially well on "Theme for Doris." On this cut Tina reaches a pitch of sorrowful eloquence, vertebrated by Art Taylor's driving beat, that lifts him for the first time to the level of the great jazz storytellers. Freddie Hubbard, then the brightest young trumpet star in New York, is an exuberant, brassy foil to the leader's musings.

Volume three, recorded a few months later and originally scheduled for release as *Back to the Tracks,* is also dominated by minor compositions. One of these, "Street Singer," cut at the same session as "Appointment in Ghana" and "Ballad for Doll," turns out, more than two decades after the fact, to have been an authentic hard-bop classic, comparable to "Caribbean Fire Dance" or "Us." Here pathos, irony, and rage come together in a performance at once anguished and sinister. Drew, Chambers, and Taylor keep the rhythm extremely taut. Against this backdrop, Tina weaves a tapestry of extended lines that lean into the beat, punctuated by soulful licks delivered in an unexpectedly keening tone. After a rather lackluster Blue Mitchell interlude, McLean steps forth with one of his most whiplike statements ever, followed by an equally "mean" contribution from Drew with a rhythmic edge comparable to Bobby Timmons's best work. Drew's style, combining funky touches with highly individual runs and figures, is one of this side's major assets. Like Hubbard's youthful exuberance on *True Blue,* it operates as a foil to Tina's looser beat on such cuts as "The Blues and I" or "The Ruby and the Pearl."

Drew is also present on volume four (Tina's last record date), along with two other under-recognized but brilliant musicians, trumpeter Johnny Coles and bassist Wilbur Ware, and another world-class drummer, Philly Joe Jones. Again, on cuts like "Dhyana" and "Stranger in Paradise," Tina shows how to construct complex, arresting solos while also wailing in the best gutbucket tradition. Thoughtful, at times melancholy and at others puckish, Coles approaches Tina's conception more than the other trumpeters on these sides. Ware, at once old-timey and avant-garde, adds an extra dimension, while Philly and Kenny smoke in their customary fashion. Philly's time is so loose it sometimes seems about to fly apart at the seams on numbers like "King David," but the center always holds, and the result is a particularly dense rhythmic texture for Tina to explore over.

Such rhythmic density, of course, was typical of hard bop, which was both close to the black popular tradition and, as it evolved, colored by a variety of musical influences (Asian, Caribbean, French impressionist). In the hands of musicians like Brooks, Morgan, and McLean, hard bop also opened up a set of emotions that in general had been little explored in jazz. These new affects, as I have noted, included defiance, bitter sarcasm, and pathos, all of which can be found on *The Complete Blue Note Recordings of the Tina Brooks Quintets,* though it is the last that dominates in Brooks's composing and playing. Like "Us" and "Caribbean Fire Dance," these records whirl us into a universe where hip street attitudes and "a tragic sense of life" intersect. Yet there are also grace and sweetness here—all played out in a context that allows jukebox values to coexist with a stringently severe aesthetic.

This was a remarkable achievement, a true fusion of black pop culture's cathartic possibilities and intense physicality with "Art" of the most demanding kind. Yet during hard bop's heyday, it was bitterly attacked by many jazz critics. Even one as sympathetic as Martin Williams, in his ironically entitled "The Funky-Hard Bop Regression," felt obliged to begin on the defensive, saying: "The gradual dominance of the Eastern and then national scene in jazz by the so-called 'hard bop' and 'funky' school has shocked many commentators and listeners. The movement has been called regressive, self-conscious, monotonous, and even contrived."[13]

These were not the only charges leveled against hard bop. As the word "hard" suggests, it gave an opening—previously uncommon in jazz—to darker emotions than we would find in Louis Armstrong or even Charlie Parker. Some jazz critics were put off by such emotions, which included wrath and bitterness. In *The Jazz Life*, Nat Hentoff comments that "among the modern 'hard boppers,' there are several musicians who have played with unalloyed hatred. 'This guy doesn't fit on the date,' one critic observed while listening to a 'hard bop' session. 'He doesn't hate enough.'"[14]

In the 1955–1965 period, *Down Beat* was the most widely read jazz periodical in the United States. Its reviewing staff included a number of critics whose views of hard bop verged on the hysterical. Preeminent among these was John S. Wilson. With incomprehensible perversity, *Down Beat* persisted in assigning Wilson many of the best hard-bop records for review. One example would be Art Blakey's *The Big Beat*, with Lee Morgan, saxophonist Wayne Shorter, Bobby Timmons, and bassist Jymie Merritt. The record bristles with such exuberant invention (among other things, it offers our first exposure to Shorter's fiery compositions) and the review is so short and dismissive that it is worth quoting in full: "Except for the opening ensemble on *Paper Moon*, this is merely a repetition of material that has been gone over time and time again by the Jazz Messengers and other groups.

"The general atmosphere is typified by *Dat Dere*, which is a mechanical repeat of something that was better the first time around.

"Morgan, Shorter, and Blakey live up to average expectations."[15]

If Wilson's attitude represented a kind of prissy squeamishness about high-voltage jazz, hard boppers were soon getting it from another angle too. In the early sixties, Amiri Baraka began publishing polemics in *Down Beat*, *Metronome*, and other journals that were designed to advance the cause of "free jazz" (Ornette Coleman, Cecil Taylor, et al.), sometimes at the expense of hard bop. Thus, in a review of *Into the Hot*, a record Gil Evans used to showcase Taylor and Johnny Carisi, Baraka remarks that "Taylor and Coleman do not have to worry about the meaningless antics of a Cannonball Adderley when there is Coltrane's continuous public confession spelling out how close to oblivion musicians like Cannonball (or Art Blakey or Bobby Timmons or the Jazztet) had brought jazz."[16]

Unfortunately, hard bop had numerous detractors and few articulate defenders; and perhaps partly for this reason, many of the critical opinions expressed above came to be accepted as received wisdom. By the late 1970s, the school no longer represented the menace it had posed in its glory days, but we find the same derogatory clichés in James Lincoln Collier's *The Making of Jazz: A Comprehensive History:* "The hard bop style was exhausted [by 1960], worn out by overuse . . . The central problem was a lack of musical intelligence, a failure of imagination on the part of the players in the style."[17]

But that wasn't generally true. In fact, the opposite could more easily be maintained: that hard bop was just hitting its stride in 1960. One thinks of such younger musicians as trumpeters Freddie Hubbard and Woody Shaw, saxophonists

Joe Henderson and Jimmy Woods, vibist Bobby Hutcherson, pianists Cedar Walton and Andrew Hill, and drummers Joe Chambers and Billy Higgins. In addition to these "new stars," many older hard boppers produced their best work after 1960: saxophonists Jimmy Heath, Jackie McLean, Harold Land, and Booker Ervin and pianists Elmo Hope and Freddie Redd, among others. Hard bop both needed and got a kind of second wind in the early sixties, and this had something to do with Ornette Coleman's rejection of conventional chord changes, but it had far more to do with developments inside the school: Miles Davis's *Kind of Blue*, Coltrane's evolution, and the influences of Thelonious Monk and Charles Mingus. These developments rescued hard bop from its own formulas, emboldening its young practitioners to cut loose and to expand what the school could encompass emotionally and formally.

[8]

HARD BOP HETERODOXY: MONK, MINGUS, MILES, AND TRANE

In André Hodeir's *Toward Jazz*, Thelonious Monk is quoted as saying, "I sound a little like [stride pianist and composer] James P. Johnson."[1] Critics have also compared Monk to such stomp-down, stride-and-blues pianists as Jimmy Yancey and Willie "the Lion" Smith. In the late forties and early fifties, Blue Note Records billed him as the "High Priest of Bebop," and he also led some classic hard-bop sessions. Two of these were *Brilliant Corners* (1956), with saxophonists Ernie Henry and Sonny Rollins; and *Monk's Music* (1957), featuring, among others, John Coltrane and Gigi Gryce. No one, however, has ever been able to pin a label on Monk. In one of his infrequent interviews, he told Grover Sales: "I'm not commercial. I say, play your own way. Don't play what the public wants—you play what you want and let the public pick up what *you* are doing—even if it *does* take them fifteen, twenty years."[2]

Born in 1920, Monk was raised on San Juan Hill, an area in the West Sixties near the Hudson River that was New York City's first black neighborhood. In the same interview with Sales, he recalled: "I learned to read notes before I took lessons. My older sister took—the girls always took in those days—and I learned to read by looking over her shoulder. Got interested in jazz right from the start. Fats Waller, Duke, Louis, Earl

132

Hines—I dug all kinds of music—liked everybody. Art Tatum? Well, he was the greatest piano player I ever heard!"[3] On his first gigs, he was a church organist and played the piano at house parties: "They used to have what they called rent parties and they used to hire me to play when I was very young. They'd pay you about three dollars, and you'd play all night for 'em. And they'd charge admission to the people who would come in and drink. That's the way some people used to get their rent together."[4]

At the age of seventeen, he toured the country with a group accompanying a preacher: "Rock and roll or rhythm and blues, that's what we were doing. She preached and healed and we played. And then the congregation would sing."[5] Barrelhouse, boogie-woogie, stride, and gospel—all these elements would resonate throughout Monk's career. Stride, for example, informs his solo on "Thelonious" on his first session as a leader for Blue Note in 1947; and gospel informs his luminous interpretation of the hymn "Abide with Me" on *Monk's Music*. His deep attachment to the black "folk" traditions, both sacred and profane, is one of Monk's links to hard bop. He revealed it long before "returning to the roots" became fashionable.

It seems a natural development that a new appreciation of Monk in the mid-fifties coincided with the rise of hard bop. Before then, he had had his champions—including Coleman Hawkins, Charlie Parker, Bud Powell, Art Blakey, and Dizzy Gillespie—but many jazzmen were put off by his "weird" conception, his technically demanding tunes, and his eccentric approach to the keyboard. Hawkins (with whom Monk did his first record date in a studio in 1944) remembered, in a conversation with Joe Goldberg, that "one of the worst things I went through in those days was with Monk, when he was working in my group. I used to get it every night—'Why don't you get a piano player?' and 'What's that stuff he's playing?'"[6] In 1955 Monk was still often ridiculed, and Orrin Keepnews of Riverside Records was able to buy his recording contract from Prestige for $108.27. But by 1957 he had virtually been canonized, and reviewers now placed him in what Keepnews called "the automatic five-star category."[7]

It also seems natural that Monk's reputation and that of Miles Davis should have risen at the same time. In fact, Davis's "comeback" was sealed by his rendition of Monk's "Round Midnight" at the 1955 Newport Jazz Festival. Both Miles and Monk reformulated the jazz tradition, returning to such basics as timbre, attack, and melody while shaking off bebop's clichés and its sometimes-calisthenic standards of creativity. Like Miles, Monk preferred to pare things down, creating an uncluttered musical space where he could work out his own solutions. In his essay on Monk in *Toward Jazz,* Hodeir mentions "the acute struggle between disjunct phrasing and those pregnant silences"[8] and declares that "only in Monk's music do asymmetry and discontinuity enhance one another, thereby assuming their full, symbiotic significance."[9]

These are matters of overall structure, but Monk was of course original in other ways too. Instead of arching his fingers (as anyone who has taken piano lessons knows all teachers recommend), he held them flat out, creating a hard, percussive sound that seemed to coax more ringing overtones from the piano than others could achieve. Monk's harmonic sense was also unique, even though his tunes were often based on conventional changes. As Alan Rosenthal observed in the *Nation:* "His chords were dissonant clusters of notes that often seemed to be groping for some sound, some sort of musical meaning, which could not be expressed on a conventional instrument. Monk once said that he would often strike two adjacent notes on the piano in an attempt to get at the note between the two. One can hear, in Monk's harmonies, this seeming attempt to express simultaneously every sound or combination of sounds made possible by its being a given moment in a given piece. Moreover, whole phrases of Monk's tunes—whole tunes, in a few cases—were without any tonal center at all. Instead, the transition from each chord to the next would create a sort of momentary or instantaneous tonality, resulting from the interaction of the two chords. Then, this tonality would change with the arrival of a third chord. In short, the listener's entire frame of harmonic reference was constantly shifting."[10]

Monk's tunes are brilliant little universes full of humor, passion, and quirkiness. His indifference to modern-jazz orthodoxy and his love affair with the past had a liberating effect on hard boppers. As Miles Davis put it: "A main influence he has been through the years has to do with giving musicians more freedom. They feel that if Monk can do what he does, they can."[11]

Exactly *how* this happened can be heard on *Brilliant Corners*, which features Oscar Pettiford and Max Roach as well as Henry and Rollins. (Paul Chambers and trumpeter Clark Terry also play on one track.) As always on Monk's dates, his personality reverberates throughout the album, encouraging everyone to extend himself individualistically and to avoid banalities. On the title cut that opens the LP, both saxophonists and Roach, challenged by the tune's eccentricity (they never did get the head quite right, and the take finally released was spliced together from various attempts) and by Monk's suggestive comping, turn in inspired performances. The raunchy, squawky theme, played first in medium tempo and then faster, leads into a Rollins solo marked by wide intervalic leaps, extended harmonies, and phrases that begin and end in unwonted places. Then Monk comes in, all minor seconds, dissonances, and idiosyncratic runs and fillips. Henry is gruff and raw, leaning heavily on his vocalized tone, from which he draws a variety of growls and slurs. The last soloist is Roach, playing melodically and even quoting the tune at times.

"Ba-lue Bolivar Ba-lues-are" is a "classic" Monk blues, at once immemorial and personal. One can feel Henry and Rollins being tugged between standard phraseology and Monk's universe. The result, in Henry's case, is a kind of bent-out-of-shape bebop, a fractured sequence of ideas, as though fragments of bop and R & B had been pasted together in a collage. Monk is calm, lucidly minimal, toying with a few elements to see how far out you can go while staying deep inside. Often he plays in duet with Roach. Rollins's warm, relaxed solo makes an effective contrast with the more strident and disquieting Henry, while Max contributes another marvelously melodic and dazzlingly polyrhythmic statement, sounding at times like a whole African percussion ensemble.

"Pannonica" is one of a series of ballads (including "Round Midnight," "Monk's Mood," and "Ruby, My Dear") in which fervent romanticism combines with Monkish astringency. After a full-blooded, rhapsodic Rollins, Monk enters on both piano and celeste, echoing one of Rollins's phrases and then dueting with himself in a solo built around variations on his own theme, whose melody he alters through subtle rhythmic and harmonic displacements. Another ballad follows: "I Surrender, Dear," one of Monk's lovingly humorous treatments of standards. The record closes with "Bemsha Swing," where Monk again bases his solo initially on the theme and then launches into a simultaneous improvisation with Roach, who plays both jazz drums and tympani on this cut. Rollins picks up Monk's last phrase and soars over the drummer's thundering accompaniment, alternating long phrases with jagged fragments. After a characteristically tart and puckish Clark Terry interlude, Roach moves to the foreground, first in duet with Monk, then alone, setting up call-and-response patterns between his two sets of tubs, and finally in duet with Rollins before the band takes the theme out.

Another composer who challenged and extended hard boppers was Charles Mingus. Equal in musical stature to Monk, Mingus was the pianist's opposite in many respects. While Monk was cryptic in his utterances, Mingus was garrulous, writing an autobiographical manuscript that ran to over a thousand pages. Monk's tunes, models of concision, were very much of a piece. Mingus's opus sprawls, ranging from forays into "classical music" to re-creations of holy-roller church services. Monk's art, in its way, was serene. Mingus's was tumultuous, boiling, seeming to chafe at the limitations of music itself. Nonetheless, the two shared several traits. Both rejected modern-jazz conventions and, drawing partly on the past (in particular the work of Duke Ellington), created worlds that set them apart from their contemporaries. They were at once more "traditional" *and* more experimental than most hard boppers. Thus, when hard bop began to seem played-out in the late fifties, Monk and Mingus each offered an alternative way of thinking, helping to save the school from the canned funk and simplistic clichés that sometimes threatened to choke it.

There are many stories of how Mingus would goad "hip" young musicians into reaching beyond their formulas. We have already seen his effect on Jackie McLean. Recalling the same period—when he and McLean were both in Mingus's band—pianist Mal Waldron told Joe Goldberg: "He makes you find yourself, to play your own style. At that time, I played a good deal like Horace Silver, and whenever I did, Mingus would be on me with 'That sounds like Horace.' . . . When I was with him, all the guys were playing very 'hip' blues, with all kinds of extra chords and passing tones. Mingus got rid of that, and made it basic. He made us play like the old, original blues, with only two or three chords, and got a basic feeling. And he brought in some gospel music too, the first time that was done. And suspensions. The way Miles and Coltrane play, getting to a particular part of a number and staying on the same chord for several bars before going on, Mingus was the first one to do that."[12]

Born in 1922, Mingus grew up in Watts, California. His first exposure to music occurred in the church he attended with his stepmother: "A lot of my music came from the church. All the music I heard when I was a very young child was church music. I was eight or nine years old before I heard an Ellington record on the radio. My father went to the Methodist church; my stepmother would take me to a Holiness church. My father didn't dig my mother going there. People went into trances and the congregation's response was wilder and more uninhibited than in the Methodist church. The blues was in the Holiness churches—moaning and riffs and that sort of thing between the audience and the preacher."[13] The Ellington record was "East St. Louis Toodle-Oo," "the first time I knew something else was happening beside church music."[14]

After taking lessons on trombone and cello, Mingus finally chose the bass, which he studied first with Red Callender and then with Herman Rheinshagen, a former member of the New York Philharmonic. Under their tutelage and through his own diligence, Mingus developed a prodigious technique. In the late forties and early fifties, he was heard in a multitude of contexts, including (for various lengths of time) the bands of Louis Armstrong, Duke Ellington, Lionel Hampton, Earl Hines, J.J. Johnson, Red Norvo, and Charlie Parker. Certain jazz bassists—Percy Heath, for example—are outstanding "walkers"; that is, they can establish solid, cushiony beats that lend tremendous rhythmic impetus to the soloists they're accompanying, while also creating harmonic density through well-chosen notes. "Walking," however, was not Mingus's specialty. Instead, he developed a freer style, both in accompaniment and in solos, that represented a step beyond Ellington bassist Jimmy Blanton's innovations in the early 1940s. Mingus's work tended toward the liberation of the bass from a subordinate role. In an excellent study of Mingus's life and work, Brian Priestley describes his vast influence on several generations of bassists playing several kinds of music: "Each of these three approaches [that can be found on Mingus's early records]—the double-stops, the octave leaps, and the subdivision of the beat by means of passing-notes—were eventually to develop further . . . But equally, they were to influence many of his successors and, ultimately, not so much through Mingus's own example but through the combined weight of all the jazz bassists he had influenced by the 1960s, they had a marked effect on the style of bass-guitar players, first in the soul field and then in rock and pop music generally."[15]

As a composer and bandleader, Mingus was equally original. He encouraged collective improvisation in his ensemble and frequently used what Mal Waldron called "suspensions" and modes instead of conventional chord changes. His shifts of tempo and mood created complexly episodic structures. All these innovations contributed to his musical legacy. In the late fifties and early sixties, his working bands were mainly composed of hard boppers. In addition to McLean and Waldron, we find trumpeters Art Farmer, Clarence Shaw, Richard Williams, Ted Curson, Johnny Coles, and Bill Hardman; and saxophonists J. R. Monterose, Ernie Henry, Shafi Hadi, Pepper Adams, John Handy, Booker Ervin, Leo Wright, Benny Golson, and Clifford Jordan. Anyone who played with Mingus learned from him. His difficult compositions and his ardent quest for new modes of expression forced musicians to play "over their heads." Many of the sidemen just named—and particularly those who stayed long enough for Mingus's lessons (and his constant hectoring) to sink in—were radically changed by the experience. He resembled Ellington in his knack for burning away what was conventional and encouraging spontaneity and inventiveness. But above all, he resembled Ellington in his range and depth as a composer. The fact that many of Ellington's best musicians stayed with him to the end—in this he had better luck than Mingus and was easier to get along with—is testimony to his ability to create a varicolored cosmos of sound beside which other music appeared monochromatic. Mingus's repertoire, too, provided a rich and elaborated context that few if any modern jazz ensembles could match. It is significant that several of his sidemen (for instance, John Handy and Clarence Shaw) never produced work outside his band to match what they had done in it.

The variety of Mingus's music and his gifts as a writer can be heard on *Mingus Ah Um*, his best-selling record and perhaps the one that is artistically most satisfying. A few years earlier, he had outlined his compositional and rehearsal methods: "My whole conception with my present Jazz Workshop group

deals with nothing written. I 'write' compositions—but only
on mental score paper—then I lay out the composition part by
part to the musicians. I play them the 'framework' on piano so
that they are all familiar with my interpretation and feeling
and with the scale and chord progressions to be used. Each
man's own particular style is taken into consideration, both in
ensemble and in solos. For instance, they are given different
rows of notes to use against each chord but they choose their
own notes and play them in their own style, from scales as well
as chords, except where a particular mood is indicated. In this
way, I find it possible to keep my own compositional flavor in
the pieces and yet to allow the musicians more individual
freedom in the creation of their group lines and solos."[16]

As a result of this approach, the musicians on *Mingus Ah
Um* sound particularly at home in the music, with a looseness
in improvising countermelodies and a layered sound that
surely comes from Mingus's methods—though the soloists'
concision was a result of careful editing after the recording
date. The band itself is a powerhouse, featuring John Handy's
sweet-and-sour alto, Booker Ervin's fiery preaching on tenor,
Horace Parlan's funky, chordal approach to the piano, and
Jimmy Knepper's avant-gutbucket trombone. It kicks off with
"Better Git It in Your Soul," a gospel-based number, mostly
in $\frac{6}{4}$ time, underpinned by driving riffs and Mingus's shouts
of "Lawd I know!" "Goodbye Pork Pie Hat" (dedicated to
Lester Young) is a lament showcasing a mournful tenor solo by
Handy that includes some effective flutter tonguing. "Boogie
Stop Shuffle," also in the minor mode, incorporates elements
suggested by its title and includes a roaring Ervin outing, while
"Self-Portrait in Three Colors" is one of Mingus's deliriously
romantic Ellington-style ballads, complexly voiced with interweaving contrapuntal lines. "Open Letter to Duke" rounds
out the first side, beginning with some of Ervin's high-octane
blowing over a shuffle beat and then segueing into a languid,
filmy ballad led by Handy's alto, another shuffle episode, and
finally a Latin vamp.

Side two starts with "Bird Calls," an up-tempo tribute to Charlie Parker, with fierce Ervin and liquid-toned Handy. "Fables of Faubus" is a loping, medium-tempo minor theme, played against a descending run on the bass. All the soloists smoke on this one; Handy is gutsy yet lithe, Parlan is sublimely bluesy, contributing a carefully constructed statement full of unexpected turns, and Ervin wails. "Pussy Cat Dues," a slow blues, offers a glimpse of Handy's clarinet playing and Knepper's dirty, deliciously vocal trombone. The album ends with "Jelly Roll," an affectionate tribute to Jelly Roll Morton that effectively contrasts an old-fashioned, bouncy two-beat with straight-ahead $\frac{4}{4}$ modern-jazz blowing.

In its abundance of memorable compositions and its multiple references to the Afro-American tradition in such varied aspects, *Mingus Ah Um* is a kind of summation of everything Mingus could do. It is also a quintessential hard-bop session, having all the qualities typical of the school: heavier use of the minor mode and strong rhythmic patterning, along with slower tempos, blues- and gospel-influenced phrasing and compositions, and sometimes lusher melodies. Mingus, of course, was as "unique" as Monk; that is, each possessed an immediately recognizable sensibility and approach. But then, that's what makes *Mingus Ah Um* a *high point* of hard bop rather than a "typical" hard-bop date.

Several years before *Mingus Ah Um* was recorded, Mingus announced in the liner notes to his *Pithecanthropus Erectus* album that he had "superimposed scales within chords and replaced bars with 'cues.'" The idea of "superimposing scales within chords"—or simply replacing conventional jazz chords with scales or "modes"—was one that a number of jazzmen were toying with at the time. Among them was composer George Russell, who had written for Dizzy Gillespie's big band and contributed two compositions ("Ezzthetics" and "Odjenar") to a Miles Davis–Lee Konitz date for Prestige in 1951. In the late 1950s, Russell was working on a modally based approach he called the "Lydian Concept of Tonal Organization."

Davis and Russell had remained friendly, and after listening to the composer explain his ideas, Miles told him: "George, if Bird were alive, this would kill him."[17]

In an interview with Nat Hentoff around the same time, Davis elaborated on his reasons for wanting to break free of standard jazz harmonies: "I think a movement in jazz is beginning away from the conventional string of chords, and a return to emphasis on melodic rather than harmonic variation. There will be fewer chords but infinite possibilities as to what to do with them. Classical composers—some of them—have been writing this way for years, but jazz musicians seldom have.

"When I want J.J. Johnson to hear something or he wants me to, we phone each other and just play the music on the phone. I did that the other day with some of the Khatchaturian scales; they're different from the usual western scales. Then we got to talking about letting the melodies and scales carry the tune. J.J. told me, 'I'm not going to write any more chords.' And look at George Russell. His writing is mostly scales. After all, you can feel the changes.

"The music has gotten thick. Guys give me tunes and they're full of chords. I can't play them. You know, we play 'Funny Valentine' like with a scale all the way through."[18]

The first fruits of this new direction were presented in the sound track for Louis Malle's film *L'Ascenseur pour l'échafaud* (*Elevator to the Scaffold*). This entire sound track was recorded in one session between midnight and dawn. The band—tenor saxophonist Barney Wilen, pianist René Utreger, bassist Pierre Michelot, and Kenny Clarke—was one Miles had been leading at the Club St. Germain in Paris. They improvised as they watched scenes from the movie, basing their solos on tonal centers and dispensing with themes and chord progressions. Although the film itself is rather insubstantial, the sound track won the Prix Louis Delluc in 1957. Miles's improvisations are alternately skittish and ominous as he meshes with Clarke's crisp brushwork on up-tempos and makes the most of his haunting tone on the slower numbers. The ad-lib quality of this music is its strength, and it has an unusually relaxed feeling. It also represents a radical break with the harmonic frameworks previously used in modern jazz.

A few months later, in April 1958, Davis was back in New York leading an expanded version of his earlier quintet. Altoïst Cannonball Adderley had joined John Coltrane in the front line, while the Red Garland–Paul Chambers–Philly Joe Jones rhythm section remained intact. The ensemble recorded a tune, called "Milestones" (or "Miles," since Davis had recorded another "Milestones" in 1947 with Charlie Parker) that again explored the possibilities of scalar improvisation. "Milestones" is based on two modes (Dorian and Aeolian) used in an A-A-B-B-A pattern. The soloists (Adderley, Davis, and Coltrane) are free to pick whatever notes they like as long as they "fit" the modes. This, of course, allows them more freedom than they would have had in a standard harmonic format, but it also deprives them of the variety such a format automatically provides. Variety, however, is built into the tune itself. In the A section, Chambers lays down a solid "walking" foundation, while Philly Joe raps out a rimshot on the fourth beat of every measure and the three horns play with bright, staccato articulation. In the B section, the phrasing is legato, Philly's rimshots are less regular, and Chambers plays a two-note figure instead of walking. The A sections sound ebullient, while the B ones have a mournful, languorous quality.

The addition of Cannonball Adderley to Miles's quintet turned the contrast between the leader and Coltrane into a more complicated, three-sided study in differences. Miles continued to hone his stripped-down, middle-register approach, which emphasized the nuances of his tone and his abilities as a melodist. Cannonball and Trane resembled each other more than either one did the trumpeter, but while Cannon was bubbly and extroverted, Trane was restless and uncompromising. "Milestones" is such a propulsive piece, however, and the

joy of discovery is so apparent in everyone's playing that these
differences between the saxes are less obvious than in other
contexts. Some of them, however, are implied in Eric Nisenson's comments on the three in his book *Round Midnight: A
Portrait of Miles Davis:* "Cannonball and Coltrane were
learning from each other, each encouraging the other saxophonist's growth and curiosity. Miles encouraged this as much
as possible, just as he had done when both Sonny Rollins and
Coltrane were in his midfifties band. When Cannonball was
playing, Miles would whisper to Coltrane, 'Listen to how
Cannonball gets in all his lyrical ideas without playing as long
as you. You should learn how to edit your ideas from him.' And
when Coltrane was soloing, Miles would tell Cannonball,
'Listen to Coltrane's harmonic ideas. You should learn to play
with his type of harmonic thinking.' After the gig, Coltrane
and Adderley would each tell the other what their boss had
said about him and laugh—they both appreciated the acceler-
ated learning experience that Miles was providing."[19]

As stunning as "Milestones" and the sound track for *Elevator to the Scaffold* had been, Miles's modal approach reached
its apogee on *Kind of Blue,* recorded in spring 1959. Again, the
band's personnel had changed. Philly Joe Jones and Red Garland had departed, to be replaced, respectively, by Jimmy Cobb
and Bill Evans. Evans, in particular, with his brooding impressionism, had great impact on the ensemble, while Cobb,
though swinging as hard as Philly Joe, was less inventive and
volatile. Actually, by the time *Kind of Blue* was cut, Evans was
also on the way out, and his replacement, Wynton Kelly, was
present at the session, though he only played on one number:
"Freddie Freeloader."

Thirty years after it was recorded, *Kind of Blue* remains, for
many, Miles's greatest single achievement. In his often-quoted
liner notes, Evans described its unusual circumstances:
"Miles conceived these settings only hours before the recording dates and arrived with sketches which indicated to the
group what was to be played. Therefore, you will hear some-

thing close to pure spontaneity in these performances. The group had never played these pieces prior to the recordings and I think without exception the first complete performance of each was a 'take.'"

The tunes, originals by either Davis or (in the cases of "Blue in Green" and "Flamenco Sketches") Evans, are masterpieces of inspired simplicity. On the first number, "So What" (in the Dorian mode), the melody is played by the bass, while the band replies with a two-note figure. Thus the mood of the album is immediately established: a blend of the blues legacy, with its bare-bones lyricism and call-and-response patterns; and the freshness of scalar experimentation. The songs that follow are a twelve-bar blues ("Freddie Freeloader"), the voluptuously wistful "Blue in Green," a waltz ("All Blues"), and "Flamenco Sketches," a ballad that, again in Evans's words, is "a series of five scales, each to be played as long as the soloist wishes until he has completed the series." If the frameworks themselves are inspired, the genius of the soloists and the contrasts among them are equally satisfying. Miles, with his blues-heavy sound, at times yearning and at others sardonic, grounds the side in a kind of jazz timelessness. Coltrane's voice is flatter and harder, harking back to his experience in blues bands yet pushing into the future through asymmetrical, arching arpeggios and cascades of sixteenth notes. Evans's solos are sketchy and introverted, almost spectral, as though his real achievement were the whole record (whose conception certainly owed much to his) rather than particular statements. And finally, Cannonball, Kelly, and Cobb concentrate on hard cooking, bringing the sound of the streets into play as a major ingredient. All these elements knit together perfectly on *Kind of Blue*, lending the record exceptional textural variety.

Not surprisingly, considering the impromptu nature of the proceedings, the musicians didn't realize quite what they had created. In an interview with Ian Carr, Jimmy Cobb recalled that "after it was over and we heard it, we went through the things . . . and it sounded so nice in the studio . . . and it

came out so good on the record . . . I said 'Damn!—it
sounded good!' But since then it got to be something special in
the music . . . a lot of people started listening to the music
with that record, and a lot of guys started to play jazz from
behind that record . . . and I had a few people tell me that
they had worn out three or four copies of that record."[20] *Kind
of Blue* would influence the course of jazz from 1959 on. Like
Monk's work and Mingus's, it was to stimulate several generations of hard boppers (including the current one), as well as
"free jazz" musicians of the 1960s, suggesting new approaches
and providing new challenges. Today, the disc has become part
of the tradition, absorbed, as unconsciously as the lungs absorb
oxygen, by young jazzmen everywhere.

In a piece published in *Down Beat* in 1960, Coltrane recalled
that on returning to Miles Davis's group after a period with
Thelonious Monk, he had found the trumpeter "in the midst of
another stage of his musical development. There was one time
in his past that he devoted to multichorded structures. He was
interested in chords for their own sake. But now it seemed that
he was moving in the opposite direction to the use of fewer and
fewer chord changes in songs. He used tunes with free-flowing
lines and chordal direction. This approach allowed the soloist
the choice of playing chordally (vertically) or melodically
(horizontally). In fact, due to the direct and free-flowing lines
in his music, I found it easy to apply the harmonic ideas that I
had. I could stack up chords—say on a C7, I sometimes
superimposed an E flat 7, up to an F sharp 7, down to an F. That
way I could play three chords on one. Miles's music gave me
plenty of freedom."[21]

As this passage implies, Coltrane was in a very different
frame of mind from Davis's. His approach was hyper-vertical.
Davis commented: "He's been working on those arpeggios and
playing chords that lead into chords, playing them fifty different ways and playing them all at once."[22] The demonic urgency of this search was clearer in live performances with
Miles—including those released on *Jazz at the Plaza, Miles*

and Monk at Newport, and *Miles Davis and John Coltrane Live in Stockholm 1960*—than on *Kind of Blue.* On the Stockholm side, in particular, we hear Trane pursuing his twin obsessions of the moment: on the one hand, to squeeze every possible implication from a song's harmonies; and on the other, to produce actual chords on the saxophone. This was a technique Monk had suggested to him: "Monk was one of the first to show me how to make two or three notes at a time on tenor . . . It's done by false fingering and adjusting your lip. If everything goes right, you can get triads. Monk just looked at my horn and 'felt' the mechanics of what had to be done to get this effect."[23]

Coltrane's playing was controversial (indeed, it remained so until his death in 1967), and it's not hard to hear why on the Swedish date. On "All Blues," for example, his solo makes concessions neither to the audience nor to the rhythm section. Wynton Kelly, normally one of the best accompanists in jazz, appears uncertain of his role behind Coltrane. What he does play often sounds fatuous, and Trane, for his part, doesn't seem to care about fitting in with the group's format. His solo *is* a kind of practicing in public, especially when he gets into his "harmonics" bag, fiddling with a couple of phrases for bar after bar as he tries to get the sound he wants from his instrument. Yet his solo also coheres, starting with simple phrases from the jazz-and-blues lexicon delivered in his penetrating tone and highlighted by guttural cries that are actually the standard use of harmonics in the black saxophone tradition. As he warms up, his phrases become longer, shading into the rapid-fire lines that Ira Gitler called "sheets of sound" and that were the vehicle for his chordal explorations. These are balanced by simpler, more "classic" figures that themselves lead into the stretch of harmonics mentioned earlier. And finally, he returns to earth in the last chorus, easing back into the standard improvisational vocabulary that had been his point of departure.

A few weeks after the Stockholm concert, Coltrane left

Miles's group for good and formed his own combo, which would ultimately include pianist McCoy Tyner, bassist Jimmy Garrison, and drummer Elvin Jones. By this time he had become the most widely imitated saxophonist since Charlie Parker. His sensibility, like hard bop itself, seemed to yoke together the world of corner bars and roadhouses and the complex preoccupations of self-conscious artists in our century. For all that Coltrane was denounced as a renegade and celebrated as a pathfinder, he had paid heavy R & B dues. In J. C. Thomas's book *Chasin' the Trane*, bassist Steve Davis remembered one of Coltrane's characteristic early gigs: "John and I worked a date in Cleveland in 1954 backing Big Maybelle. The club owner wanted John to walk the bar, but John just looked down and patted his stomach, saying, 'Sorry, I've got ulcers.' We cracked up and the club owner got hostile, until our guitarist, Junior Walker, offered to walk the bar because he had an extra long cord from his guitar to the amp. He did it while John played some wailing blues behind Big Maybelle. She was so pleased she told the audience, 'John Coltrane is my favorite musician, and you'd better believe it, because that's the truth.' "[24]

Other jobs were with Eddie "Cleanhead" Vinson, Gay Cross (formerly with Louis Jordan), Earl Bostic, and Bull Moose Jackson—not to mention Jimmy Smith ("Wow. I'd wake up in the middle of the night and hear that organ. Those chords screaming at me").[25] Despite some work with Johnny Hodges, Dizzy Gillespie, Howard McGhee, and Bud Powell, Trane, by the time he joined Miles Davis in 1955, had played much more R & B than jazz in public. The head-shaking, finger-popping physicality of R & B would remain an essential element in his style, grounding it in an intensely social, communicative, and cathartic music.

At the same time, in the late fifties, Trane was studying. He would spend hours a day working on scales and harmonies, trying to get them to "lie under his fingers" to the point where they could emerge naturally in his solos. His months in

Thelonious Monk's quartet at the Five Spot Café, where jazz-men, poets, painters, and bohemians in general flocked to find out what was happening at the cutting edge of hard bop, were especially important: "Working with Monk brought me close to a musical architect of the highest order. I felt I learned from him in every way—through the senses, theoretically, techni-cally. I would talk to Monk about musical problems, and he would sit at the piano and show me the answers just by playing them. I could watch him play and find out the things I wanted to know. Also, I could see a lot of things that I didn't know about at all."[26]

All these influences, plus Miles Davis's ("He also made me go further into trying different modes in my playing"),[27] con-verge in Coltrane's style on a tune like "Chasin' the Trane," recorded in 1961 with bassist Reggie Workman and Elvin Jones. In the liner notes accompanying the record (*Coltrane Live at the Village Vanguard*), the saxophonist explained that "usually, I like to get familiar with a new piece before I record it, but you never have to worry about the blues, unless the line is very complicated. In this case, however, the melody not only wasn't written but it wasn't even conceived before we played it. We set the tempo, and in we went."

"Chasin' the Trane" is a sixteen-minute solo, but in another sense it is really a duet with Elvin Jones, whose interactive drumming swirls around, above, below, and behind the beat as he dialogues with Trane. The proceedings are anchored by Workman's robust walking bass and by Coltrane's deep empa-thy with the blues. Trane takes elemental phrases and turns them upside down, playing them all kinds of ways, transposing and fragmenting them. You can hear him thinking as he improvises, yet the result is anything but aridly "experimen-tal." Trane's forward-driven rhythmic sense and his hot, pierc-ing sound make this as relentless a performance as one can find on a jazz record. In Frank Kofsky's *Black Nationalism and the Revolution in Music*, Coltrane called the jazz-and-blues tradi-tion "a big reservoir, that we all dip out of."[28] Here the reservoir is not only in these elemental blues phrases but in the tonal effects that fill his solo. His experiments with harmonics, so evident on "All Blues," have now been reabsorbed to the point where they are no longer experiments but another electrifying timbral effect to go with his honks and screams. Likewise, all those hours of practicing scales and harmonic exercises have now been assimilated, so that whereas "All Blues" modulates out of the tradition into first "sheets of sound" and then harmonics, "Chasin' the Trane" gives the primal and the sophisticated to us all at once.

By 1961, Ornette Coleman had hit the scene, and the "free jazz" movement was shaking up a generation steeped in hard bop's certainties, irritating some and inspiring others. Coltrane was obviously among those inspired, but rather than dispense with fixed harmonies as Coleman had done, he sought to stretch them as far as he could. As Martin Williams remarked, Coltrane was "prepared to gush out every conceivable note, run his way a step at a time through every complex chord, every extension, and every substitution, and go beyond that by reaching for sounds that no tenor saxophone had ever uttered before him."[29] Thus, for the generation of hard boppers coming of age in the early sixties, Coltrane was more of a model than Coleman could be. Coltrane was the sound of hard bop revitalizing itself, sloughing off everything rigidly formulaic, seeking out new modes of expression while retaining the school's mixture of high-modernist self-awareness and hipness. Eventually, Coltrane would abandon musical "hipness" altogether, but this development was still several years in the future. In the meantime, along with Miles, Mingus, and Monk, he epitomized jazz's amalgam of the earthy and the exalted, galvanizing a new generation of musicians with his achievements.

CHANGES

In *Blues People,* which remains one of our most provocative studies of jazz, Amiri Baraka declares that by 1960 "hard bop, sagging under its own weight, had just about destroyed itself as a means toward a moving form of expression."[1] This is an exaggeration (and, indeed, the author goes on to say that hard boppers like John Coltrane, Sonny Rollins, and Elvin Jones "emerged in the sixties working in new areas"), but one does understand what he means. As the 1950s drew to a close, a certain sameness crept into hard bop, both in public performances and on the records issued by Blue Note, Prestige, and other labels. The tunes were too perfunctory and banal, and solo styles had become increasingly formulaic. Rollinsoid saxophonists and Clifford Brownoid trumpeters; overuse of flatted fifths on the piano; simplified, squared-off bebop and blues-and-gospel clichés trotted out for the millionth time were symptoms of rigor mortis setting in. Horace Silver had dipped into the styles of Pinetop Perkins and Jay McShann, but when young pianists began copping them from Silver (tapping the "wellsprings of black music" at a considerable remove), one knew something was amiss. Hard bop was feeding on itself. As Elmo Hope put it in 1961: "The fellows out here need to do a little more exploring. They should delve more in creativity instead of playing the same old blues, the same old funk, over and over again."[2]

Yet hard bop was also under pressure to change, and musicians *within* the school moved to burst its constraints. In addition, Ornette Coleman's 1959 arrival in New York City fissured the jazz world as had nothing since bebop. Coleman was hailed by many—and particularly by a number of critics— as a genius, a true original, a "new Charlie Parker." Others, however, felt that far from moving beyond conventional harmonies and the chromatic scale, he had simply never mastered them. Coleman's music, at once revolutionary and atavistic, charged with the raw cry of the blues (he had paid as much dues on the "chitlin' circuit" as any boss tenor), left no one indifferent. How deeply Coleman shook even the most idiosyncratic hard boppers can be heard in Mingus's comments in a 1960 interview: "Now aside from the fact that I doubt he can even play a C scale . . . in tune, the fact remains that his notes and lines are so fresh. So when Symphony Sid played his record, it made everything else he was playing, even my own record that he played, sound terrible. I'm not saying everybody's going to have to play like Coleman. But they're going to have to stop playing Bird."[3]

Few hard boppers actually converted to Coleman's brand of music. Many, however, were influenced by it directly or indirectly—and especially indirectly. Coleman redefined the outer limits of jazz, making anyone less iconoclastic seem relatively "conventional." Coltrane, for example, who in the early sixties was being reviled by some for playing "anti-jazz," was at the same time being urged by more avant-garde critics to break, once and for all, the umbilical cord tying him to chord changes and modes. Compared to Coleman, he was conservative; and within a few years he did in fact abandon fixed harmonies.

Another eminent hard bopper who responded to Coleman's music was Sonny Rollins. In 1959, Rollins had retired from jazz temporarily and, in Leonard Feather's words, had entered "a period of self-imposed exile during which he re-assessed his values, investigated Rosicrucianism, and practiced assiduously, often in the solitude of the pedestrian walk of the Williamsburg Bridge, high above the East River."[4] His first gigs and his first record date after his return in 1961 sounded much like his previous work, but in 1962 he put together a band with trumpeter Don Cherry and drummer Billy Higgins, both of whom had played with Ornette (a few months earlier Coltrane had also hired a bassist, Jimmy Garrison, who had been working with Ornette).

Leading this band, Rollins made a record (*Our Man in Jazz*) that represents a kind of culmination of his previous work. Despite what one might have expected, the group is certainly rooted in hard bop. Rollins sounds like his former self, and both Cherry and Higgins had extensive modern-jazz credentials. Yet the record leaves one feeling that everything eccentric, original, and exploratory in Rollins's post-1955 production was here taken to its logical consequences.

His tone is a bit drier, more sinewy than it had been. His time is even looser, his references to bebop vocabulary more oblique. A tune like "Oleo," which occupies an entire side, opens with an up-tempo cascade of tumbling phrases interspersed with deep-funk figures and half-time passages. Cherry follows Rollins's lead with sensitive obbligatos that sometimes build into simultaneous improvisations. About halfway through this cut, a descending, Ornettishly bluesy secondary theme is introduced, eventually kicking off another Rollins solo that turns what had been a breakneck chase into a laid-back medium tempo. Higgins follows the sax's lead till it eases into a loping duet with Cherry's mournful riffs. Having lowered the temperature, Rollins then starts building again. Quotes abound, seeming to function as historical references— for example, to Wardell Gray's "Twisted Blues." Of all the jazz records ever made, this is one of the few that truly capture the atmosphere of free interaction, the spontaneity of the best live performances.

At the time of its release, *Our Man in Jazz* was taken as a
sign of Rollins's defection to the free-jazz camp. Though it
remains one of the peaks of his career, it proved to be merely an
episode in his development. The association with Cherry and
Higgins didn't last long, and afterwards Rollins returned to a
more conventional style. The side stands, however, both as a
sign of Ornette's intensely magnetic attraction and as an
indication of how pointless the bebop versus free-jazz contro-
versy was essentially. Rollins, Cherry, and Higgins could and
did play in both modes, and this was true as well of most young
jazzmen who emerged in the early sixties.

Jackie McLean also responded to jazz's altered landscape. In
the liner notes to his *Let Freedom Ring* album, he confessed
that "getting away from the conventional and much overused
chord changes was my personal dilemma. Until recently this
was the reason why many of the things I composed in 1955 left
me helpless when it came to a basis for improvisation, for
example, 'Quadrangle' and 'A Fickle Sonance.' Both of these
tunes were just recently recorded. I used 'I Got Rhythm' for the
solo section in 'Quadrangle.' These changes do not fit the
personality of the tune at all. Today when I play 'Quadrangle,' I
use sections of scales and modes. I try to write each thing with
its own personality. I choose the outstanding notes of the
composition and build a scale or a motif to fit the feeling of the
tune. Today I am going through a big change compositionwise,
and improvising. Ornette Coleman has made me stop and
think. He has stood up under much criticism, yet he never
gives up his cause, freedom of expression. The search is on."

Let Freedom Ring does represent a breakthrough for
McLean, though in a way that resembles Coleman less than
these comments suggest. In the background one hears John
Coltrane's and Miles Davis's modal experiments, and some
aspects of Trane's evolving improvisational style—yet even
so, what takes place falls far short of wholesale appropriation.
All the elements of McLean's previous approach remain present, including his unmistakably soulful sound and his blues-

and bebop-based phrasing, but others have been added. He uses the alto's lower register—and its "freak" upper register above the normal upper register—to brilliant effect. At times he flattens his tone. Modes rather than chord changes dominate, and in general the side bristles with excitement and the thrill of discovery. Like *Our Man in Jazz*, it benefits enormously from Higgins's relaxation, his rattling commentaries on the solos, his kaleidoscopic accents and cross rhythms.

To call *Let Freedom Ring* McLean's most scorching album is to say a lot, considering the incandescent quality of most of his playing; but this recording seemed to catch him on a day when he was especially ready to blow his heart out. Of the four tracks, three are dedicated to members of his family—his mother Alpha Omega, his son René, and his daughter Melonae—and one to Bud Powell, Jackie's first mentor, who had been caught in the toils of madness since the early 1950s. This tune is one of Bud's most poignant compositions, the minor-keyed ballad "I'll Keep Loving You." In a moving tribute to its composer, McLean plays a solo as concentrated and free of extraneous clutter as any Ben Webster recorded. The tune is topped off by a breathtaking out-of-tempo rendition of the theme in which McLean first blows hard, using the "freak" upper register to build intensity, and then softens his sound to a wispy sob.

Another high point on the LP is "Omega," which McLean described as "in two sections. The outside is built on an F# major mode and is free of tempo, to a degree. The second section swings along with a happy feeling."[5] Actually, the first section is no more "free" than the second, but the tempo is varied by alternation between a patterned vamp, underscored by an ascending bass figure and Higgins's cymbals, and a more straight-ahead section. McLean's blowing is perhaps his loosest on the date, as he shakes off a lot of bebop grammar, phrases more personally than usual, and again employs all his horn's registers in this joyously shimmery performance. Walter Davis, Jr., who previously had been known as a good journeyman bebop pianist, also obviously felt liberated by the proceedings and displayed a more orchestral style in his solos than he had before.

Around the same time that he cut *Let Freedom Ring*, McLean formed a working unit that included three of the most talented younger musicians around: vibist Bobby Hutcherson, trombonist and composer Grachan Moncur III, and the remarkable seventeen-year-old drummer Tony Williams. All of them were firmly rooted in modern jazz—Moncur via J.J. Johnson, Hutcherson via Milt Jackson, and Williams via Roy Haynes and Elvin Jones—but they were also attracted to the "new thing," which they both played and drew upon in their work as hard boppers. Though Moncur was the weakest soloist, his compositions and use of the combo's original instrumentation contributed much to its special character. The band recorded three albums for Blue Note—*One Step Beyond*, *Destination Out*, and *Evolution* (this last under Moncur's name). All were very good, but *Evolution* was perhaps the best, partly because Lee Morgan was added to the quintet.

As with the other albums just mentioned, the title of *Evolution* proclaims these musicians' exhilarated sense of adventure. They truly *were* evolving, a process underlined in liner notes by A. B. Spellman, one of free jazz's main advocates: "My initial reaction to this record—the first representation on LP of Grachan Moncur's work as composer and leader—was surprise. I'd expected to hear a hip, hardbopping, J.J. Johnsonesque trombonist leading a band with like bent thru tunes as familiar as the IND subway line, but what I got was a serious and courageous date composed out of an audacious interest in the more open methods of solo and group improvisation, in the kind of playing that's already been declared anathema by the more conservative factions of the jazz world . . . Men like Moncur, Hutcherson, Williams, & Cranshaw are part of what I have called the second wave of the avant-garde in that they, with such radicals from the preceding generation as Jackie McLean and John Coltrane, form a bridge between the outcast revolutionists and the mainstream. Their ears are wide open; they are technically prepared to execute the most demanding and abstract parts; their professional and social involvement with more traditional musicians keeps their historic reference in front of them, but their interest in what can be done in musical self-assertion forces them to constantly alter the rules, which is about the most commercially dangerous thing a musician can do; and, best of all, because so many of the more talented young musicians are falling in with them, they are undeniable."

All four tunes on *Evolution* are Moncur originals. The first, "Air Raid," consists of two parts: one out of tempo and the other medium-up. The slow segments, dominated by bassist Cranshaw's glissandi and Hutcherson's undulating tremolos, seethe with the kind of dramatic menace implied by the title. The faster interludes are fueled by Williams's prodigiously inventive drumming, a tempest of controlled sound and fury. Over all this atmospheric turbulence, McLean creates a collage of fragmented bebop, elliptical snips and wisps of phrases he leaves dangling, allowing the listener to fill in the empty spaces. Morgan also contributes a riveting solo, biting and precisely articulated on up-tempos, languidly bluesy on slower ones, which ends with a quote from "Blues in the Night" ("my mama done tole me") that seems to anchor Moncur's experiments in the earliest jazz.

The other tunes are equally memorable. "Evolution" is a stately, out-of-tempo, modal dirge: a two-note melody played over shifting internal voicings and punctuated by Williams's funeral-march rolls. "The Coaster" is a sort of avant-flagwaver, fired up by repeated riffs and building to Morgan's hotblooded solo. And finally, "Monk in Wonderland" switches between $\frac{3}{4}$ and $\frac{4}{4}$ time signatures, using a Jazz-Messengerish shuffle beat on the latter. All the musicians make the tempo transitions gracefully (how far we had come from the stiff experiments with jazz waltzes only a few years before!), gliding elegantly over the song's shifting beat and generally having a ball. It's not surprising that Morgan later remembered the date as an important moment in his development.[6] Everyone met the challenges posed and was propelled beyond himself on this electrifying session.

McLean, Morgan, and Rollins were not alone. With varying degrees of fanfare, most of hard bop's "stars" and popular combos found inspiration and renewal in the early sixties. Tony Williams's drumming, for example, became a key factor in Miles Davis's band. Horace Silver combined modal structures and Latin rhythms on *The Tokyo Blues*, his most cohesive album since *Further Explorations*. He then went on to hire two young turks for his new quintet: tenor saxophonist Joe Henderson and trumpeter Woody Shaw, both of whom could play "outside" and "inside," as musicians put it at the time. After Silver's departure from the Jazz Messengers in 1956, that combo had seemed to flounder for several years as later units tried to get by without a composer who could give their repertoire an overall shape. This problem was solved briefly in 1958 by Benny Golson's stint, but it was vanquished much more definitively when Wayne Shorter joined in 1960. For the next few years, Shorter's trenchant-yet-melancholy themes galvanized two outstanding ensembles: the first with Lee Morgan, Bobby Timmons, and bassist Jymie Merritt; and the second with Freddie Hubbard, Curtis Fuller, Cedar Walton, and Reggie Workman, in addition to Blakey and Shorter.

And as with Blakey, Davis, and Silver, so it went with any number of less celebrated musicians. Jazzmen and aficionados, for instance, had always valued trumpeter Kenny Dorham's sharply syncopated phrasing, full of subtle rhythmic displacements, as well as his tart, dark tone and austerely motif-oriented solos. Dorham was never a killer technically in the manner of Dizzy Gillespie or Clifford Brown. But along with Miles Davis and Art Farmer, he had helped define an area of melodic invention and tonal nuance that greatly broadened the trumpet's range of expression. He now teamed up with Joe Henderson for a series of records, some under his own name and others under Henderson's, that reflected his openness. As he put it: "If you keep on living, you have to keep on growing. That is, if you keep your feelings and your ears open."⁷ Dorham had clearly remained responsive to new sounds, and his compositions on these discs used changing tempos and unusual bar structures and chord sequences.

Dorham, Henderson, Blakey, Hubbard, Hutcherson, McLean, Morgan, Shorter, and Silver all recorded for Blue Note Records, which dominated the jazz scene—or at least this aspect of it—as it never had before. Blue Note proved to be extraordinarily supportive of new developments in hard bop and, as Alan Rosenthal comments, its musicians "did seem to use the label freely and extensively as a laboratory situation in which to try out all the variable aspects of their music . . . The result of this broadening of horizons was that in the years immediately prior to 1967 the 'Blue Note sound' continued to be characteristic in stylistic ancestry [hard bop] and in instrumentation but ceased to be limited in scope. Perfection seemed imminent. In albums like Joe Henderson's *In 'n' Out*, Larry Young's *Unity*, and Wayne Shorter's *Speak No Evil* (and many others), one hears the unmistakable extending of jazz's profoundly physical embrace to encompass the complexities and anxieties of modern life, not in the primitive 'out of the mouths of babes' way that swept Ernest Ansermet off his feet when he heard Sidney Bechet in 1919, but with a conscious awareness of those complexities and a determination to prevail over and even transform anxiety through sheer force of swing."⁸

Of all Blue Note's "new stars," perhaps the most intriguing was pianist Andrew Hill. I first encountered his work in fall of 1963. I had returned home from Maury's Met Record Mart, one of those ghetto jazz specialty shops once so common and now virtually extinct, clutching a copy of altoist Jimmy Woods's *Conflict.* The album as a whole proved to be one of the most ferocious hard-bop releases ever. Though all the musicians played with originality, I was especially struck by Hill, whom I had never heard of. His percussive attack and jagged lines seemed to leap forth from the record, announcing the arrival of a major new keyboard stylist.

Hill, who then stood on the verge of a remarkable outpouring of creative energy over the next two years, had grown up in Chicago, where he attended the University of Chicago's Lab School. In an interview with Leonard Feather, Hill recalled his first musical experiences: "I started out in music as a boy soprano, singing, playing the accordion and tap dancing. I had a little act and made quite a few of the talent shows around town from 1943, when I was six, until I was ten. I won turkeys at two Thanksgiving parties at the Regal Theater. The parties were sponsored by the *Chicago Defender*, a newspaper I used to sell on the streets of Chicago.

"In 1950 I learned my first blues changes on the piano from Pat Patrick, the baritone saxophonist . . . Three years later I played my first real professional job as a musician, with Paul Williams' rhythm and blues band. At that time I was playing baritone sax as well as piano."[9]

Gigs followed with such Chicago stalwarts as tenor saxophonists Gene Ammons, Von Freeman, and Johnny Griffin and bassists Israel Crosby and Wilbur Ware, as well as with a variety of jazzmen passing through the Midwest. These included Miles Davis, Charlie Parker, and Lester Young; and during this same period, Hill made friends with Barry Harris, whom he would later claim as an influence along with Thelonious Monk, Bud Powell, and Art Tatum. In addition to practicing Monk's, Powell's, and Tatum's solos till he knew them by heart, Hill studied composition: "A friend of mine named Eddie Baker was taking lessons from William Russo. I took a few lessons with him too. Then I sent a composition to Hindemith at Yale that allegedly had maturity beyond my years. When Hindemith came to Chicago, I went to see him and he showed me things about extended composition during the five times or so that I saw him over a two-year period."[10]

After this initial burst of activity, Hill retired from the

music scene for three years, which he spent studying "more serious things—books."[11] He returned to public performance leading a trio that nailed down some of the best gigs in Chicago, cut an album for Warwick Records, and in 1961 accompanied Dinah Washington to New York. There he performed in a number of contexts, playing on vibist Walt Dickerson's rhapsodic *To My Queen* album, backing up singers Johnny Hartman and Al Hibbler, and appearing as a sideman with Kenny Dorham, Clifford Jordan, Rahsaan Roland Kirk, Jackie McLean, and the Johnny Griffin–Lockjaw Davis quintet. Late 1962 and early 1963 found him on the West Coast, accompanying Howard Rumsey's and Kirk's ensembles and recording with Jimmy Woods. He soon returned to New York City, however, and shortly thereafter (in September 1963) played on one of Joe Henderson's Blue Note records with Kenny Dorham. Alfred Lion, the label's co-director, was impressed by Hill's work and signed him to an exclusive contract.

What followed was a series of tremendously original recordings of great emotional power. Though Hill seemed—at least to New Yorkers—to have sprung into being full-grown, those who had heard him earlier in Chicago described a rather conventional pianist whose playing was more a pastiche of standard effects than a volcano of individuality. Lion, perhaps regretting his earlier parsimony with Thelonious Monk (who recorded only ninety minutes of music in his five years with Blue Note), brought Hill into Rudy Van Gelder's studio three times in three months. *Black Fire*, Hill's first Blue Note LP, was cut in November 1963. *Smokestack* followed a month later, and *Judgment* a month after that. *Point of Departure*, his best-known album, was done in March 1964; *Andrew!* dates from June 1964. Even today, 95 percent of Hill's reputation rests on these five albums, all recorded within an eight-month period.

In the liner notes to *Black Fire*, Hill is quoted on the subject of his three pianistic teachers (five if you count Ravel and Debussy): "Monk's like Ravel and Debussy to me, in that he's

put a lot of personality into his playing, and no matter what the
technical contributions of Monk's music are, it is the personality of the music that makes it, finally. Bud is an even greater
influence but his music is a dead end. I mean, if you stay with
Bud too much, you'll always sound like him, even if you're
doing something he never did. Tatum, well, all modern piano
playing is Tatum."

In a sense, modern-jazz piano playing may well derive from
Tatum. But Tatum as a specific influence is hard to detect in
Hill's music, nor is Powell much easier to find. There is a
parallel with Monk in that Hill's world is instantly recognizable and stamped with a singular vision and set of musical
coordinates. Temperamentally, however, the two pianist-
composers are far apart. For one thing, Monk's music is often
good-humored, while Hill's is about as solemn as you can get
in jazz. Hill's playing is simultaneously tormented and cerebral, two adjectives rarely applicable to Monk. Monk's borrow-
ings from the popular and jazz traditions have mostly to do
with the 1930s, a decade Hill makes scant use of. No artist
exists outside his own time, and Hill is clearly a modern-jazz
pianist, but his main stylistic antecedents cannot be found
among the pianists of the 1940s.

To understand Hill, one must look toward hard bop, both as
it crystallized in the playing of musicians like Elmo Hope and
Mal Waldron and in a more general sense, as a style and
emotional stance. Like Hope's and Waldron's, Hill's playing
has a somber, driven quality. His tunes, like theirs, tend to
favor the minor mode. Dissonance, insistent use of seconds,
obsessively repeated phrases, asymmetrical melodic lines, and
empty space employed as a structural element are all points of
comparison. Many of Hill's compositions (like "Land of Nod"
on *Black Fire*, "Catta" on Bobby Hutcherson's album *Dia-
logue*, or "Siete Ocho" on Hill's *Judgment*) are typical hard-
bop numbers in several respects, including their quasi-Latin
flavor and a sinister air, easy to recognize but harder to define,
known as "badness."

In addition, Hill's classical background makes itself felt in subtle and complex ways. His initial flurry of Blue Note dates, as it happened, coincided with "third stream music," an insipid hybrid despite the involvement of artists like pianist-composer John Lewis. What Hill seemed to take from the European tradition, however, had little to do with such middlebrow pablum. Instead, he drew upon the sort of feelings and postures that Alan Rosenthal calls "complexities and anxieties." These had begun to creep into jazz with bebop (and even more with hard bop) but had rarely been appropriated so directly and wholeheartedly. "Sinister, brooding, cerebral, angst-ridden, intellectually restless"—how many of these words could be applied to any jazz prior to 1945? And how much qualification would they need with most beboppers? Powell, however, was an exception in some ways and fit the profile better than his peers. Classical music, then, may have functioned for Hill and for a number of others (for example, Elmo Hope) as an invitation to venture—or venture further— into affective realms relatively unexplored by their predecessors.

With such examples around and behind him, Hill set about creating his own music. Standard jazz licks were so rare in his initial recordings that they stood out emphatically. One of the most percussively alive of pianists, Hill used a bassist (Richard Davis, aided by Eddie Khan on *Smokestack*) and drummers (Joe Chambers, Roy Haynes, Elvin Jones) who could create dense, polyrhythmic textures for him to work with and against. As much as any African master drummer, Hill relied on first-rate accompaniment to orient himself rhythmically. This symbiosis is particularly clear if we compare his interactions with Roy Haynes and Elvin Jones. Haynes tends to push the time, and Hill responds by holding back; Jones plays a little behind the beat, and Hill tugs against him too, pushing things forward to maintain the same rhythmic tension we find with Haynes. Cascading runs; rolling triplets; punched-out, repeated, transposed two-note chords and phrases all form part of

Hill's melodic vocabulary. So does his eccentrically fragmentary phrasing, which violates bar lines even more than bebop did. Hill's harmonic sense brought him close simultaneously to the atmosphere of much previous hard bop, to Monk in certain respects, and to the French impressionists he cited in the same breath as his favorite jazz pianists.

Any of Hill's initial Blue Note releases could be discussed as an example of his work in the early sixties. *Smokestack,* however, is possibly the most suitable, if only because it consists solely of Hill, bassists Khan and Davis, and Haynes. Khan generally stays in the background, soloing only once and laying down an unobtrusive line behind Davis's far more aggressive contributions, which range from inspired obbligatos to veritable duets with the pianist, as on the ballad "Verne." Every tune is an original, as was the case on all of Hill's early LPs. *Smokestack's* one up-tempo cut is the title track, where an exceptionally busy rhythmic-harmonic texture churns and swirls around Hill, who sometimes cuts against and at other times rides the rhythm section's ebb and flow. Intricately voiced, ringing chords alternate with tumbling runs and licks lifted from blues vocabulary and demonically hammered out on medium-tempo tunes like "The Day After," "Ode to Von," and "Not So." Through it all, Haynes and Davis surge in and out of the foreground, complementing Hill, filling whatever gaps he leaves, and displaying an exquisite alertness both to each other and to the pianist. Perhaps the most striking piece on the record is "Wailing Wall." There, over the tide of Haynes's cymbals and sputtering traps, Hill's lush chords, and Khan's walking bass, Davis creates a bowed solo described by Don Heckman as "a long declamatory line that moves sensuously in and out of semitone and microtone changes of pitch."[12] Another high point is "30 Pier Avenue," a slow rocker free of all the clichés we usually associate with this genre and yet as soulful after its fashion as anything Jimmy Smith ever played.

Critical reaction to Hill's first five Blue Note releases was unanimously favorable, though for entirely different reasons with different critics. A. B. Spellman, who wrote the liner notes to *Black Fire*, praised Hill's intrepid avant-gardism as opposed to what he called "a sickening familiarity about the jazz mainstream." Leonard Feather, on the back of *Judgment*, took an opposite tack, congratulating the pianist for his closeness to the jazz tradition and avoidance of "nihilism" (presumably a reference to Ornette Coleman, Cecil Taylor, and others championed by Spellman). Yet despite all this variously motivated praise, five-star reviews in *Down Beat*, and a steady stream of new releases, Hill performed infrequently in public. Although he had previously worked in a wide variety of contexts, he now turned down gigs in others' groups, remarking to Nat Hentoff that "when you become a piano player in someone else's band, you have to adopt that band's style, and I feel that I'm in a period during which I have to grow by myself."[13] Hill seemed to think of himself as another Thelonious Monk, waiting for the world to catch up with him and determined not to compromise his artistic standards. Meanwhile, Blue Note's Alfred Lion—and later, Frank Woolf—went on recording Hill regularly, apparently convinced of his genius. All told, according to Michael Cuscuna, he recorded "eighteen or nineteen" albums for the label between 1963 and 1971.[14]

Andrew Hill stopped being a significant presence in the world of night clubs (where most live jazz is played) after the early sixties. In 1968, he declared that he had been "living off the generosity of patrons—composing, practicing and now really thinking about starting to perform more often again."[15] Instead, however, he took a position as composer-in-residence at Colgate University between 1970 and 1972, during which time he also earned a Ph.D. in composition. From 1972 to 1975, he participated in the Smithsonian Institution's touring program together with his wife, Laverne. In 1975 he moved to California: first to San Francisco and then in 1977 to Pittsburgh, some sixty miles away. There he performed in churches and concert halls, participated in musical therapy programs in prisons like Soledad and San Quentin, and worked in the schools.

Hill's success in maintaining his involvement with music while avoiding the pressures and challenges of the jazz life has not been matched by the quality of his production. After his first spate of recordings, he ventured into free jazz with a release entitled *Compulsion*. The record, which features a standard jazz quintet augmented by a second bassist and two percussionists, is a dismal failure. It is muddy in texture, pretentious, full of pseudo-exotic effects and aimless noodling despite the excellence of the musicians (Freddie Hubbard, tenor saxophonist Johnny Gilmore, bassists Cecil McBee and Richard Davis, and Joe Chambers). Hill must have thought better of this direction, for we soon see him attempting an old-fashioned, straight-ahead hard-bop album (*Grass Roots*) with Lee Morgan, Booker Ervin, bassist Ron Carter, and drummer Freddie Waits. But again, despite the caliber of the sidemen, the record is a disappointment. Hill's solos sound diffuse, as though his mind were elsewhere, and the drive, focus, and edge of his earlier playing are absent. The side includes an inept and blatantly commercial groove number called "Soul Special." "The Rumproller," a Hill composition featured on Lee Morgan's follow-up to *The Sidewinder*, was another failed attempt at popular success. In 1969 Hill recorded a disc entitled *Lift Every Voice*, on which he was backed by a chorus, and another with strings, issued as *One for One*.

These efforts, one is sorry to say, were neither commercially nor artistically successful. The late sixties were not propitious years for such undertakings, as R & B displaced jazz from black jukeboxes the two styles had previously shared. Moreover, the "popular touch" is one of the muses' more special gifts. Not every outstanding jazz musician can produce a tune like Horace Silver's "Song for My Father," at once a musical creation of great charm and a natural hit. Hill, for all his brilliance, lacked this particular knack—as did Powell, Tatum, Monk, and most major jazz pianists.

Hill's musical groping and disintegration, unfortunately, were matched by many of the Blue Note regulars. Hard bop, which had entered the sixties so exuberantly, was moribund by the end of the decade. Why this happened and what exactly *did* happen—as well as the possible future of jazz in an era of virtual invisibility in black neighborhoods—are the subjects of the next chapter.

10

THE LAST OF HARD BOP

There's no live name jazz to speak of in Atlantic City nowadays. But thirty or forty years ago there were all *kinds* of things going on—not only there but in dozens of other American towns. Harry A. Reed's "The Black Bar in the Making of a Jazz Musician: Bird, Mingus, and Stan Hope" describes the jazz clubs of that era: "First, the clientele, at least those attending the sessions, came to listen, not to dance. They were a musically hip audience that could appreciate the nuances of fine playing. Additionally, spectators played an active role in encouraging young players. Not only did they clap enthusiastically but also they shouted, talked to soloists, snapped their fingers and created an appreciative, critical, and interactive atmosphere. The fact that the listeners were not primarily dancers was tremendously liberating to the young jazzmen, for they felt no necessity to learn popular tunes with repetitive beats attuned to dance rhythms."[1]

Reed goes on to recall the clubs in Atlantic City, where he was initiated into the music and watched his friend Stan Hope develop into a professional pianist: "Since Atlantic City was convenient to New York and Philadelphia, it was then a magnet for hopeful black musicians. The larger clubs, both black and white, and the Steel Pier booked big bands and well-known small groups to attract the tourist trade. In the years 1948 through 1955, a typical week might have the Count Basie band, Tadd Dameron's Orchestra, Earl Bostic, and Chris Powell's Five Blue Flames featuring Clifford Brown, all playing in town. Simultaneously, smaller big-name groups would be booked into certain smaller clubs: Dizzy Gillespie, Milt Jackson, Lester Young, Jimmie Smith, and Sonny Stitt. Lesser-known musicians from the New York State and Pennsylvania areas would augment this talent supply. Preeminent among this latter group were tenorman Morris Lane, guitarist and vocalist Billy Butler, and drummer Coatsville Harris. Finally, local musicians such as pianist Stan Hope, drummer Sid Trusty, bassist Donald Watkins, and others would fill out this talent pool. In short, a ready supply of musicians and a range of bars existed to provide a laboratory for exploring musical ideas."2

Though Reed was talking about the period just before hard bop, I myself encountered a somewhat similar world in Chicago in the early 1960s: a cornucopia not only of jazz but of urban blues, soul, and gospel. By 1970 this world—or at least its jazz and blues components—had vanished. Again in Alan Rosenthal's words: "The 'rock explosion' and the mass exodus of black listeners from more commerical types of jazz to R & B resulted in an almost complete sealing off of club gigs, airplay, and record dates to jazz musicians. The effect was economically and psychologically devastating. It was almost as though jazz had had a stroke in late 1967. Even just a few years later, in the early '70s, it was referred to in a few prominent places where it was beginning to be nurtured again as a music whose 'comeback' was urgently to be desired."3

This "devastation" was felt most acutely by the young up-and-coming hard boppers of the early sixties. In 1962, Freddie Hubbard had told Ira Gitler: "This is a thing I want to stay in for life. I don't want to joke about it. 'Cause if you're not doing what you really want to do, you're never going to be satisfied . . . I mean I want to make money—everybody does—

but I'm not going to go in any certain direction for money."[4]
Ten years later, Hubbard was recording blatantly commercial,
excruciatingly banal albums as he tried to position himself in
the fusion/jazz-rock/crossover scene. In 1981, covering Hubbard's return to jazz pure and simple, Stanley Crouch remarked that "for the past year or more, Hubbard has expressed
weariness, if not revulsion, with his attempts at superstardom,
reiterating a desire to start playing real music again."[5] Yet
Hubbard's work since 1981 has not regained the sparkle and
grace of his playing in 1964.

The attrition rate in modern jazz had always been very high.
Bebop began in 1945, but within a decade most of its major
figures were dead (usually of drug addiction) or out of commission. Artistic burnout—even without crippling vices or aesthetic wrong turns—has not been uncommon. Sooner or later,
a young musician must lose some of the fire and audacity of his
early playing and (one hopes) replace it with a mellower, more
thoughtful style. Some hard boppers have known how to make
this transition; many haven't. Even more than other artists,
jazz musicians as improvisers are on the spot. What they create
is fragile, and their genius must constantly be proven anew.
Anyone who tires of the effort or settles into a style based on
his own clichés has lost his creative edge.

Fortunately for the music, there always seemed to be an
inexhaustible supply of young jazzmen to replace the fallen—
again, until the late 1960s. As Jackie McLean recently recalled:
"I felt it and that's why I moved out of New York. One of the
reasons I wasn't reluctant to move out of New York in 1969,
1970 when I moved out, [was] because there was a real void in
the music in terms of young people going after it like we used
to go after it, Sonny Rollins and all of us when we were kids,
Arthur Taylor. I couldn't find those kids, and I was in education. They weren't available."

Why did this happen? The answers are complicated, and the
question has been asked not only by jazz fans but by lovers of
blues and rawer forms of R & B (which today sound even more

anachronistic to young blacks than does jazz). On the one hand, we have seen the homogenization of the music business on all levels, from the disappearance of mom-and-pop record stores to the charting of "megatrends" by conglomerate record companies. Television has been a mighty leveler of autonomous cultures of every sort. The collapse of black ghettos as viable cultural contexts—partly due to the decline of discrimination in housing, which dispersed working and middle-class blacks and left the subproletariat to stew in its own juices—has been an additional factor. Prior to the 1960s, it is true, black neighborhoods were segregated racially, though not as all-black as they would be after the riots. But they were remarkably integrated in terms of social class, for professionals and others with steady jobs were forced to live cheek by jowl with the lumpenproletariat. Indeed, this story and its cultural consequences are as old as jazz, which was born in New Orleans partly as a result of interaction between two groups. One consisted of mulattos schooled in European music but deprived of their special status by the Jim Crow laws of the late nineteenth century. The other consisted of men who played a rawer, "blacker" style but lacked the mulattos' formal polish. When these two groups were thrown into contact—or so the legend goes—jazz was born.

In the late 1960s, the reverse occurred. According to Jackie McLean, young people who earlier might have become jazz musicians now were affected by "the way the commercial music was taken and the onslaught of the Beatles and Rolling Stones and all the groups like that that just turned it around. I mean, the black community didn't follow the Beatles that much. A lot of the kids, when we began to have a black middle class and you found black families moving away from the centers of black culture, the Harlems and the inner city here in Hartford, moving out in West Hartford and Bloomfield up this way, those kids naturally interacted with the middle-class white kids, so their musical standards and mores changed somewhat."

As had happened in the late 1940s and early 1950s, the weakness of jazz around 1970 coincided with a robust and innovative black popular music that siphoned off at least as much of its audience as the Beatles and Rolling Stones had done. This music drew on a variety of sources, including jazz but also rock. The new work introduced "concept albums," lyrics that were more intimate than before but also hipper and more realistic, and greater harmonic subtlety. These were among the elements in soul music's broadened range. Jazz had previously been considered the most sophisticated, demanding, intellectually supple product of black musical culture. But by the early 1970s, this point had become questionable. Albums like Stevie Wonder's *Music of My Mind*, Marvin Gaye's *What's Going On* and *Let's Get It On*, Curtis Mayfield's superb sound tracks *Superfly* and *Claudine* (the latter featuring Gladys Knight and the Pips), as well as Norman Whitfield's collaborations with the Temptations were arguably more interesting in every respect and particularly—in relation to what preceded them—more daring than anything happening in jazz.

The ferment in soul music naturally caught the attention of jazz's hemorrhaging black audience. Despite some dubious generalizations and his ignorance of jazz, Simon Frith gives a good overall picture of this shift in *The Soul Book:* "Affluent blacks (middle-class and well-off workers, suburb not street people) had always had unsettled tastes in music. Basic black forms—blues and R & B and gospel—were too basic, too rough and emotional in content and place, too redolent of hard pasts and feared futures. This audience needed elements of prosperity and elegance and style. For a long time they found them in jazz, being the main supporters of jazzmen and jazz clubs, but the introspective styles of the late fifties were *too* uninvolving and left the audience looking elsewhere for comfort and fun. They discovered soul: the brassy jazz soul of Cannonball Adderley, Ray Charles and their slicker successors; the sweet soul fusion of blues and gospel of Sam Cooke, the Impressions and the Motown acts.

"But during the sixties this affluent audience began to experience and react to the same changes that affected young whites and the ghettos. As they became more aware and assertive of their blackness, soul music seemed to be getting whiter—whether teenage white of the Top Ten groups or show-biz white of the *Ebony* stars. But the new black music was not theirs either—it was too rough, too much in awe of ghetto values and ghetto vices and ghetto myths. The Temptations' new music was just what was needed: it was black, it was funky, it was soulful—and it was adult, complex and cool. Whitfield's achievement [in tunes like "Cloud Nine" and "Papa Was a Rollin' Stone"] was not exactly to make street music respectable (one contrast to rough) but to make it sophisticated (another contrast to rough) and this had musical as well as social significance. The affluent black audience was an audience of stereo owners and LP buyers; they spent their nights in small clubs, not huge halls; their musical expectations were formed by jazz as much as pop. The new Temptations, as compared to, say, James Brown, went down like a good red wine as compared to corn whiskey."[6]

What was jazz offering at the same time? To an unfriendly observer, the answer would be Miles Davis's neurotic noises on *Bitches Brew*, Pharoah Sanders's cheap incense, and stale bebop. Moreover, with few exceptions—like Donald Byrd's work with the Blackbirds—"crossover" and "fusion" meant jazz plus rock rather than jazz plus soul. Perhaps a fusion with soul was impossible. The music was too singer oriented, and jazzmen weren't about to give up their hard-won places in the spotlight. On the other hand, there were some excellent soul instrumental groups—for instance, the Bar-Kays—and Marvin Gaye made good use of jazz arrangers like J.J. Johnson and Bobby Scott and instrumentalists like pianist Joe Sample and saxophonist Ernie Watts. Gaye, Wonder, Mayfield, et al. knew how to use jazz—and especially hard bop, up to and including the advances of Miles Davis and John Coltrane—but jazzmen didn't know what to do with "soul," even though they had introduced the term. Instead of defending their access to the audience described by Frith, many either aimed their efforts at white teenagers or retreated into a bland, vaguely jazzy muzak that lacked personality of any sort. If fusion with soul would have been difficult, fusion with rock and the more anemic sorts of pop was musically degrading.

At about this time, some interesting offshoots of "free jazz" were growing more visible. Much like hard bop (though without hard bop's rigorous standards of proficiency), it had been a sprawling, varicolored movement. Alongside charlatans who couldn't play were stylists of real genius. Often all they had in common was ostracism by the now moribund "jazz mainstream." From Sun Ra's kaleidoscopic performance art to Steve Lacy's ascetic probings to Archie Shepp's reformulation of the big-toned Swing-tenor tradition, the movement bristled with creative energy while at the same time allowing entry to practically anyone who owned an instrument.

What was needed was a little discipline. And to some extent, help was provided by two midwestern collectives: the Chicago-based Association for the Advancement of Creative Musicians (AACM, founded in the early 1960s), and its St. Louis counterpart, the Black Artists' Group (BAG, founded in 1968). The fact that pianist and composer Muhal Richard Abrams co-founded the AACM was a sign of new astringency, since Abrams could play in any style, had impeccable hard-bop credentials, and certainly knew the difference between experimentation and noise. Among those who emerged from or helped form the AACM were trumpeter Lester Bowie, trombonists Joseph Bowie and George Lewis, saxophonists Roscoe Mitchell and Henry Threadgill, and drummers Steve McCall and Philip Wilson. BAG was responsible for three quarters of the current World Saxophone Quartet (Hamiet Bluiett, Julius Hemphill, and Oliver Lake). All these musicians had excellent chops. They were voraciously eclectic, absorbing elements of Latin and "exotic" musics, ragtime and marching bands, avant-garde classical music, and gutbucket blues. They made joyous, disconcerting, unpredictable music, and when they descended on New York City in the early 1970s, they caused considerable commotion on the "loft jazz" scene. They didn't win back jazz's audience, but they put out some terrific sounds. Like Mingus and Monk, they disdained rigid notions of "hipness" and reached deep into jazz's past while also apparently suggesting its future.

Jazz's future in the 1980s, however, proved to be quite different. The music did make something of a comeback, but among whites more than among blacks. One wouldn't want to overstate the case—after all, classical orchestras playing the nineteenth-century symphonic repertoire are far more generously subsidized than is jazz—but in a modest way, jazz began to get some government and foundation support, along with considerable airplay on public radio. There was a flood of reissued records, covering every period of jazz history (but especially hard bop) and bringing huge chunks of the repertoire back within reach of listeners. Independent jazz labels again appeared, and major companies like CBS, Capitol, and RCA started active jazz programs. History of jazz courses became popular at universities. For young whites, jazz was once again "hip," and older people bored with rock also embraced it. There have even been some jazz films, including *Round Midnight*, which starred Dexter Gordon, and Clint Eastwood's *Bird*. Jazz is back. In *Desperately Seeking Susan*, a 1980s movie about a bunch of cool young artsy types in Soho, one character's loft is burglarized. His first question is: did they get his Charlie Parker sides?

Here Charlie Parker functions as an icon—as indeed he did in life and has ever since his death. As Bob Reisner remembered: "To the hipster, Bird was a living justification of their philosophy. The hipster is an underground man. He is to the second World War what the Dadaist is to the first. He is amoral, anarchistic, gentle, and overcivilized to the point of decadence . . . His [Bird's] death was felt powerfully in these circles. For days and weeks afterwards, on sidewalks and

fences I saw a crude legend written in chalk or crayon, BIRD
LIVES. To the hipster Bird was their private possession."[7] That
was Bird in his own time. And today, what kind of complicated
nostalgia (complicated because it's a second-hand nostalgia for
an era one never knew) could he evoke in a twenty-year-old?
As many years have passed since Bird's death as between the
beginnings of recorded jazz and his death.

Today, for many listeners, jazz is indeed a nostalgia trip, and
the boundary between celebrating jazz and embalming it is not
always very clear. Still, young musicians, some of them very
good and others very promising, continue to play the music.
But particularly if they are black—and virtually all the great
jazzmen have been black—they can no longer pluck it from the
air but have to come by it more circuitously. Thus Wynton
Marsalis, the most praised young trumpeter of the 1980s,
declared: "I know if it weren't for the fact that my father [New
Orleans pianist Ellis Marsalis] is a jazz musician, for the fact
that he has jazz records, I know that I would not play jazz,
because there was nothing. None of my surroundings, none of
my peers, nothing on the radio, nothing I got at school gave me
any input."[8] And tenor saxophonist and bass clarinetist David
Murray recently characterized the kind of music that *is* available in black neighborhoods: "Well for one, they got the blaster
in their ear and they got it on the wrong stations. It's peer
pressure. A guy turns on a jazz station and the kids say, 'Aw,
man, turn it off, put on Kool Moe Dee or something.' Some
kids don't listen to anything that's not a rap. I think it's kind of
a drag that a kid won't listen to a whole song that's instrumental all the way through. They want to hear that slave beat."[9]

Marsalis has emerged as something of a spokesperson for a
group of neo-boppers who have made their mark in the last few
years. Perhaps his clearest statement of how he sees himself
came in an interview with Francis Davis: "No, see, when I first
came to New York in 1979, everybody was talking about
fusion. Everybody was saying that jazz was dead because no
young black musicians wanted to play it anymore, and because

the established cats who should have been setting an example were *bull*shittin', wearing dresses and trying to act like rock stars. So when people heard me, they knew it was time to start takin' care of business again. I wasn't playing shit no one had ever heard before, but at least I was playing some real music."[10]

Marsalis first came to most listeners' attention through his work with Art Blakey's Jazz Messengers. He went on to become a star at the head of his own combos, which have often included his brother Branford on tenor and soprano saxophones. After Marsalis's departure, Blakey assembled another band featuring young modern-jazz traditionalists from New Orleans: trumpeter Terence Blanchard and saxophonists Donald Harrison and Jean Toussaint. Blakey, of course, was one of the inventors of hard bop, which his ensembles continued to play, but the term "hard bop" fell into disuse as musicians and listeners conflated it with bebop. Nonetheless, Marsalis, Blanchard, and company tried to go back to the fifties and sixties, bypassing free jazz and fusion, reestablishing contact with a tradition they feel was broken and that had produced especially subtle and demanding music. The danger, as many have noted, is that hard bop in their hands will become a "period style" to be "re-created." As Blanchard commented: "Part of trying to play jazz and being young is—I have all the records, I've listened to so many things that when I start playing my first reaction is, 'Oh, that's not what Clifford Brown would play, that's not what Miles would play, let me stay away from that.'"[11]

These young musicians' work was not innovative, and as a result many critics responded not so much with condemnation as with a kind of queasy faint praise. In an article entitled "In Jazz, Young Players Turn to the Old Hard Bop," Jon Pareles remarked that Marsalis's pianist Marcus Roberts "never threatens to go out on a limb, much less to shake foundations. But his revivalism lends his music a sense of security, of sanctuary, that may be as prized in our times as hard bop's

exploratory outreach was in the 1960's."[12] And in "The Return
to New Orleans," Gary Giddins's take on the school was that
"considering the pervasive influence of Miles Davis's quintets
on these musicians, I'm not sure there's anything indigenously
Southern about this flurry of New Orleans talent—except
perhaps for the uncommonly skillful musicianship that pre-
cedes their quest for originality. Judging from their liner comments, they aren't especially concerned with being original,
and they are quick to catalogue the particular lessons of
particular masters. They approach jazz with refreshing detach-
ment, as though it were a music to be mastered and not a
spontaneous revelation of soul. How novel."[13]

To which Terence Blanchard indirectly replied: "That's also
part of the problem of people looking at young jazz musicians
and saying, 'They aren't playing anything new.' They haven't
even given us a chance to develop."[14] Well, fair enough, but
most of the jazzmen Blanchard admires developed individual
styles early on. In Chapter 3, I listed some of the best hard-bop
pianists of the 1950s: Ray Bryant, Sonny Clark, Kenny Drew,
Tommy Flanagan, Elmo Hope, Wynton Kelly, Herbie Nichols,
Horace Silver, Mal Waldron, and Randy Weston. None of them
was an "innovator" in the sense that Art Tatum had been, but
they all were individuals with easily recognizable styles. It's
one thing not to want to storm the heavens and push back the
frontiers of jazz, and most jazzmen haven't been interested in
such a quest. But it's another to put together such a bland
pastiche of Herbie Hancock, McCoy Tyner, and Cedar Walton
(or of Miles Davis and Freddie Hubbard) that nobody can tell
who's playing.

If critics have shown caution in evaluating the neo-boppers,
musicians like Henry Threadgill have sometimes been more
forthright: "Music doesn't come out of a vacuum. It's connected to the whole fabric of life. I don't believe that you can
escape the influence of your times—you can't fabricate the
feelings and social connections of another period. For the first
time in the history of jazz, many young artists have become

virtuosos of styles that have passed. A lot of people have taken the wrong slant, working on being technically proficient, but technique is supposed to be a given; unless it's innovative, don't bother me. Are we so nostalgic that we need virtuosos of the graveyard?"[15]

Threadgill's own music is also full of references to the past, but he doesn't try to re-create any particular style. A member of the Chicago AACM, in the early sixties he played in a sextet that included bassist Malachi Favors and saxophonists Joseph Jarman and Roscoe Mitchell (all members of the Art Ensemble of Chicago), as well as behind blues vocalist Mighty Joe Young, gospel singer Jo Jo Morris, and several Latin bands. In 1971, together with bassist Fred Hopkins and drummer Steve Mc-Call, Threadgill formed Air. Air evolved into one of the most original and intriguing groups in jazz. Constant rehearsals produced a rare integration of written and improvised material (often you couldn't tell which was which) and helped the three musicians develop a sublime and almost eerie attunement to each other. For the last few years Air had been inactive, and Threadgill has turned his attention to larger ensembles: in particular, a septet that nonetheless goes by the name of the Henry Threadgill Sextett.

A lot of Air's material—mostly composed by Threadgill—was too "free" for the finger-popping segment of the jazz public. The Sextett, in this sense, is more "accessible." Threadgill's voicings are often sourly brassy in the manner of old-time street bands, and his charts conjure up all kinds of ghosts from American popular music's past: New Orleans funeral marches, fanfares, heavy-groove blues, calypsos, even a number ("Award the Squadtett" on *Easily Slip into Another World*) that sounds like a football anthem. The brass players—at first trumpeter Olu Dara and trombonist Craig Harris; later trumpeter Rasul Siddik and trombonist Frank Lacey—possess vocally inflected styles reminiscent of the twenties and thirties and complete with growls, wah-wah effects, and a whole set of dirty-trombone tactics. The band is anchored by two drummers, Fred Hopkins's booming bass, and Deirdre Murray's cello. Its particular quality, however, comes from Threadgill's compositions, which combine irony and passion, re-creating the rowdy pandemonium of the AACM but channeling it into performances that also swing mightily. In its appropriation of jazz's "roots," Threadgill's group suggests hard bop, and particularly Mingus's reach into the past and his slightly bugged-out reworkings of Ellington. Threadgill is too complex to pin one label on, but his work definitely tilted toward the tradition in the late 1980s. So did that of the World Saxophone Quartet, which in addition to Bluiett, Hemphill, and Lake, included David Murray. The WSQ began as an every-man-for-himself affair, and its early performances were rather shapeless. Within a few years, however, it had evolved into one of the smoothest, freshest sounds in jazz: a creamy choir by turns funky and swooningly Ellingtonian (again!). In fact, two of its records featured Ellington tunes in one instance and rhythm and blues in the other. The AACM-based Art Ensemble of Chicago also became somewhat more traditional in the late 1980s. Even so, no one would ever confuse Threadgill, the WSQ, or the Art Ensemble with the neo-boppers, whose idea of *usable* tradition is more restricted.

Why did groups like Threadgill's reorient themselves toward groovier sounds? One reason was probably money. Free jazz never brought large financial returns, and perhaps they got tired of playing for small audiences and small change. In addition, in some cases there was a change of heart. As David Murray put it: "I like to swing and swinging brings out the best in most people. It has to be listenable. You know how we used to play; the drummer would never play ¼. But if a guy comes out and plays that way now, in the eighties, the people start walking out. On a positive musical plane, I love to swing, I think I can swing, I just need to find the right people to swing with."[16] Murray's comments also imply financial motives (no club owner is likely to hire a group that drives away customers)

and a sense that times had changed and jazz's climate was
more conservative. Still, Murray, Threadgill, and company
were definitely living in the present; no one was likely to
confuse their music, for all its historical awareness, with the
products of some earlier period.

Murray's love of swinging was always evident, but the
overall formats of his tunes, their rhythms and harmonies,
moved closer and closer to hard bop. His earliest musical
experiences in California could hardly have been more funky:
the Murray Family Band, a gospel group including his parents
and two brothers; and the Notations of Soul, a fifteen-piece
revue he co-led as a teenager with pianist Rodney Franklin.
Murray's conversion to jazz was sparked by hearing Sonny
Rollins perform at a jazz festival. Since then he has learned
from many other tenor saxophonists, ranging from Swing
titans Paul Gonsalves and Ben Webster to the avant-garde. For
a time after his arrival in New York City in 1975, he was an
active participant in the loft-jazz scene. In the eighties, however, he worked in more tightly organized contexts: a big band,
a string ensemble, his quartets and octets, and the WSQ. With
the exception of the WSQ (a cooperative ensemble whose
charts were mostly written by Julius Hemphill), these groups
combined exploratory solos using free jazz but not confined to
it with Murray's catchy, melodically appealing compositions.

Among these combos, perhaps the one that most clearly
shows Murray's direction in the 1980s is his octet, whose most
celebrated record, *Home*, features Olu Dara, cornetist Butch
Morris, Henry Threadgill, pianist Anthony Davis, bassist
Wilbur Morris, and Steve McCall. All these musicians paid
dues on the free-jazz scene, none has renounced its advances
and innovations, but all can acquit themselves admirably in
more straight-ahead situations. Side one begins with "Home,"
a ballad carried by muted brass and Threadgill's flute. Like
many of Threadgill's own compositions, it seems to echo the
work of Charles Mingus. This is followed by "Santa Barbara
and Crenshaw Follies," a high-spirited, contrapuntal, bluesy

strut; and "Choctaw Blues," a good-natured appropriation of
Hollywood's notion of an Indian war dance, underlined by
McCall's rolling-thunder mallets. Side two is devoted to two
longer cuts: "Last of the Hip Men," a modal number using
vamps and an implied Afro-Caribbean beat; and "3D Family,"
a waltz leaning heavily on blues-and-gospel riffs to build
intensity. Though these tunes are freshly and interestingly
voiced, they also respect and rejoice in jazz's conventions and
establish solid grooves for the musicians to work in. Murray
doesn't hog the spotlight, but his solos dominate the record.
His broad, swaggery sound, punctuated by penetrating honks
and false-register squeals, soars and swoops over the rhythm
section in an outpouring of undulating lines, yet there is
melody and rhythmic precision here too. He brings the entire
history of the tenor sax, from Coleman Hawkins to Albert
Ayler, into play, while making you feel that its future is
ensured as long as young musicians can create with so much
authority.

While hard bop can be heard in bands like Murray's and
Threadgill's, there's no point overstating its influence on their
music. It's there, along with other elements, as one aspect of
jazz's history to be combined with the others. As for the neo-
boppers, they do have the chops to create great music, and their
diligent apprenticeship in the tradition may yet bear fruit. Jazz,
as Marsalis and Murray make clear, has not regained its
standing in black neighborhoods. Perhaps it never will, but
while talented musicians play it, it will endure and evolve. As
Art Blakey, leader of some of the fieriest young bands in jazz,
recently remarked: "[Jazz] isn't as widespread, but [young
musicians] are closer than they ever were, and it's better
because you don't need the majority to conquer. You get just
twenty of them that's strong enough to hold together and you
can go through anything."

NOTES

1. Bebop

1. New York: Doubleday, 1979; repr. New York: Da Capo Press, 1985, 145, 146.
2. New York: MacFadden Books, 1962, 9, 10.
3. Ibid., 54, 55.
4. Reproduced in Roy Carr, Brian Case, and Fred Dellar, *The Hip: Hipsters, Jazz and the Beat Generation* (London: Faber and Faber, 1986), 13.
5. New York: William Morrow and Company, 1963, 188.
6. New York: Macmillan, 1966; repr. New York: Da Capo Press, 1984, 208.
7. *Howl and Other Poems* (San Francisco: City Lights Books, 1956), 9.
8. *Jazz Masters of the 40s*, 264.
9. Ibid., 263
10. Cited by Chris Whent in liner notes to *The Dizzy Gillespie Story Volume Two: The Champ*, Realm 118 (issued in London in 1963).

2. Hard Bop Begins

1. "Andrew Hill's Alternative Avant-Garde," *Village Voice* (30 Oct. 1984), 93.
2. This and other details of *Billboard*'s charts can be found in two

books, both edited by Joel Whitburn: *Top LPs 1945–1972* and *Top Rhythm and Blues Records 1949–1971* (Record Research: Menomonee Falls, WI, 1973).

3. New York: Horizon Press, 1960; repr. New York: Da Capo Press, 1983, 101.
4. Joe Goldberg, *Jazz Masters of the 50s* (New York: Macmillan, 1965; repr. New York: Da Capo Press, 1983), 70.
5. Nat Hentoff, "An Afternoon with Miles Davis," in *Jazz Panorama*, ed. by Martin Williams (New York: Crowell-Collier, 1962; repr. New York: Da Capo Press, 1979), 168.
6. Nat Hentoff, *The Jazz Life* (New York: Dial Press, 1961; repr. New York: Da Capo Press, 1975), 208.
7. Booklet accompanying *The Complete Blue Note and Pacific Jazz Recordings of Clifford Brown*, Mosaic MR5-104, 2.
8. *Jazz Masters of the 50s*, 94.
9. "A Tribute to Brownie," *Down Beat* 23:17(22 Aug. 1956):10; repr. in booklet accompanying *The Complete Blue Note and Pacific Jazz Recordings of Clifford Brown*, 5.
10. Ibid., 1.
11. Gitler, *Jazz Masters of the 40s*, 271, 272.
12. "A Tribute to Brownie," in Mosaic booklet, 5.
13. *Four Lives in the Bebop Business* (New York: Pantheon Books, 1966), 192.
14. *Jazz Masters of the 50s*, 91.
15. Repr. in *Jazz Panorama* as "Sonny Rollins and Thematic Improvising," 239.
16. Goldberg, *Jazz Masters of the 50s*, 59.
17. Nat Hentoff, "Jazz Messengers Blazing a Spirited Trail," *Down Beat* 23:4(22 Feb. 1956):10.
18. *Mister Jelly Roll* (New York: Grosset and Dunlap, 1950), 62.
19. "Jazz Messengers Blazing a Spirited Trail," 10.

3. A New Mainstream

1. This statement was printed on the back covers of "Mainstream" records produced by Stanley Dance for the Felsted label in the late 1950s.
2. This and the following three quotations are from "Michael Ullman on Jazz: Horace Silver," *The New Republic* 179:2 & 3(July 8 & 15, 1978):32.
3. *New York Times Magazine* (16 June 1985),45.

4. *Jazz Masters of the 50s*, 74, 75.
5. *The Jazz Life*, 210.
6. Liner notes to *Full View*.
7. New York: Horizon Press, 1976; repr. New York: Da Capo Press, 1987, 211.
8. 28:1(5 Jan. 1961):16.
9. *Down Beat* 27:25(8 Dec. 1960):42, 44.
10. This quotation and the following one are from the liner notes to *Sonny Clark Trio*, Blue Note BST-81579.

4. The Scene

1. Private letter to the author, 13 June 1986.
2. *The Jazz Life*, 68.
3. Ibid., 69.
4. New York: Collier Books, 1988, 58.
5. Repr. in *Jazz Panorama*, 272.
6. *Down and In*, 84.
7. Repr. in *Advertisements for Myself* (New York: Signet, 1960), 305.
8. 86.
9. *Advertisements for Myself*, 313.
10. New York: Freundlich, 1984, 163.
11. 85.
12. 92.

5. The Lyricists

1. Englewood Cliffs, N.J.: Prentice Hall, 1988, 192.
2. "Barry Harris: Interview," Bob Rusch, *Cadence* $\frac{7}{8}$:12(Dec. 1977):18.
3. Gitler, *Jazz Masters of the 40s*, 89.
4. "Art Farmer: Interview," *Cadence* 10:5(May 1984):10.
5. No. 144(Jan.-Feb. 1976):3,4.
6. "Farmer's Markets," *Down Beat* 25:12(12 June 1958):18.
7. Ibid.
8. "A New Jazz Corporation: Gryce, Farmer," *Down Beat* 22:21(19 Oct. 1955):10.
9. Ibid., 11.
10. Liner notes to *Art*, Argo LPS-678.

11. Liner notes to *Art Farmer Quintet at Boomers,* Inner City IC 6024.
12. Harry Frost, "Benny Golson," *Down Beat* 25:10(15 May 1958):19.
13. Ibid.
14. "Perspectives," *Down Beat* 25:1(9 Jan. 1958):34.
15. Liner notes to Benny Golson, *Blues on Down,* 2-Milestone 47048.
16. "Poet," *The New Yorker* (24 Feb. 1986):80, 81.
17. "Michael Ullman on Jazz: Tommy Flanagan," *The New Republic* 180:16(21 Apr. 1979):26.
18. Whitney Balliett, "Tommy Flanagan," *The New Yorker* (20 Nov. 1978):204.
19. Ira Gitler, "Kenny Burrell," *Down Beat* 30:17(1 Aug. 1963):23.
20. "Tommy Flanagan," 204.
21. "Barry Harris: Interview," 18.
22. "Tommy Flanagan," 203.
23. "Motor City Classicist" in *Rhythm-a-ning: Jazz Tradition and Innovation in the '80s* (New York: Oxford Univ. Press, 1985), 126.

6. Tenors and Organs

1. Leonard Feather, *From Satchmo to Miles* (Briarcliff Manor, N.Y.: Stein & Day Publishers, 1972; repr. New York: Da Capo Press, 1984), 108.
2. This quotation and the two others from Reig that follow appear in Robert Palmer's liner notes to *Honkers and Screamers: Lee Allen, Big Jay McNeely, Hal "Cornbread" Singer, Sam "The Man" Taylor, Paul "Hucklebuck" Williams,* Savoy SJL 2234.
3. Arthur Taylor, *Notes and Tones: Musician to Musician Interviews* (New York: Perigee Books, 1982), 67.
4. Don De Michael, "Focus on Johnny Griffin," *Down Beat* 28:1(5 Jan. 1961):20.
5. John Shaw, "Lockjaw Davis: A Musician Who Matters," *Jazz Journal* 23:9(Sep. 1970):10.
6. "Jaws Unlocks: Vern Montgomery in Conversation with 'Lockjaw' Davis," *Jazz Journal International* 36:7(July 1983):14.
7. "Lockjaw Davis: A Musician Who Matters," 10.
8. "Jaws Unlocks: Vern Montgomery in Conversation with 'Lockjaw' Davis," 14.
9. Pete Welding, "Jaws and Johnny," *Down Beat* 28:13(22 June 1961):21.

10. This and the following quotation from Turrentine are in "Pete Hamill on Jazz: Don't Mess with Mr. T," *New York Daily News*, Leisure Section (14 Aug. 1977):3.
11. Ibid., 4.
12. For example, *Down Beat* 27:17(18 Aug. 1960):17.
13. "Introducing Stanley Turrentine," *Jazz Monthly* 7:5(May 1961):7.
14. "Lockjaw Davis: A Musician Who Matters," 11.
15. Harvey Siders, "Jimmy Smith: A New Deal for the Boss," *Down Beat* 37:20(15 Oct. 1970):15.
16. This quotation and the following one are from Leonard Feather, "Jimmy Smith: Jazz Organist," *International Musician* 70:10 (Apr. 1972):6.
17. Quoted by Leonard Feather in "Jimmy Smith: Jazz Organist," 6, 17.
18. "The Electric Organ in Jazz—Jimmy Smith and Some Others," *Jazz Monthly* 7:11(Nov. 1961):12.
19. Liner notes to Jimmy Smith, *A New Star—A New Sound*, Blue Note BST 81512.
20. Dan Morgenstern, "Mellow McDuff," *Down Beat* 36:9(1 May 1969):19, 20.
21. "Mellow McDuff," 19.

7. The Power of Badness

1. "Pete Hamill on Jazz: Don't Mess with Mr. T," 13.
2. Quoted by William Dufty in liner notes to *The Billie Holiday Story*, MCA2-4006E.
3. Don De Michael, "Identifiable Lee," *Down Beat* 28:4(16 Feb. 1961):16.
4. Quoted by Michael Cuscuna, "The Blue Note Story," Blue Note Records December 1988 catalogue, 9.
5. Ibid., 8.
6. *Four Lives in the Bebop Business*, 213.
7. "A Progress Report on Jackie McLean," *Jazz Monthly* 8:5(May 1962):5, 6.
8. Gary Giddins, "The Return of Jackie McLean," *The Village Voice* (11 Aug. 1975):92.
9. *Four Lives in the Bebop Business*, 216.
10. Quoted in Leonard Feather's liner notes to *Jackie's Bag*, Blue Note BST-84051; CDP-46142.

11. Quoted by Michael Cuscuna in booklet accompanying *The Complete Blue Note Recordings of the Tina Brooks Quintets*, Mosaic MR4-106.
12. Ibid.
13. Repr. in *The Art of Jazz* (New York: Oxford Univ. Press, 1959; repr. New York: Da Capo Press, 1980), 233.
14. 140.
15. 27:21(13 Oct. 1960):35.
16. Repr. in *Black Music* (New York: William Morrow and Company, 1973), 107.
17. Boston: Houghton Mifflin Company, 1978, 452.

8. Hard Bop Heterodoxy: Monk, Mingus, Miles, and Trane

1. New York: Grove Press, 1962; repr. New York: Da Capo Press, 1986, 166.
2. "I Wanted to Make It Better: Monk at the Blackhawk," *Jazz: A Quarterly of American Music* No. 5(winter 1960):38.
3. Ibid., 34.
4. Les Tompkins, "The Classic Interview: Thelonious Monk," *Crescendo International* 24:6(June 1987):12.
5. Hentoff, *The Jazz Life*, 194.
6. *Jazz Masters of the 50s*, 28.
7. Ibid., 33.
8. *Toward Jazz*, 177.
9. Ibid., 171.
10. "The Music of Thelonious Monk," 219:8(21 Sep. 1974):248.
11. Hentoff, "An Afternoon with Miles Davis," *Jazz Panorama*, 167, 168.
12. *Jazz Masters of the 50s*, 138, 143.
13. Hentoff, *The Jazz Life*, 161.
14. Quoted by Diane Dorr-Dorynek in liner notes to *Mingus Ah Um*, Columbia CJ-4-0648; CK-40648.
15. *Mingus: A Critical Biography* (New York: Quartet Books, 1983; repr. New York: Da Capo Press, 1984), 25, 26.
16. Liner notes to *Pithecanthropus Erectus*, Atlantic SD-8809; 8809-2.
17. Eric Nisenson, *Round About Midnight: A Portrait of Miles Davis* (New York: Dial Press, 1982), 148.
18. "An Afternoon with Miles Davis," 167.

19. 156.
20. Quoted in Ian Carr, *Miles Davis: A Biography* (New York: Quill, 1984), 108.
21. John Coltrane with Don De Michael, "Coltrane on Coltrane," *Down Beat* 27:20(29 Sep. 1960):27.
22. "An Afternoon with Miles Davis," 165.
23. "Coltrane on Coltrane," 27.
24. New York: Doubleday, 1975; repr. New York: Da Capo Press, 1976, 66, 67.
25. August Blume, "An Interview with John Coltrane," *The Jazz Review* 2:1(Jan. 1959):25.
26. "Coltrane on Coltrane," 27.
27. Quoted by Nat Hentoff in liner notes to John Coltrane, *Giant Steps*, Atlantic SD-1311; 1311-2.
28. Frank Kofsky, *Black Nationalism and the Revolution in Music* (New York: Pathfinder Press, 1970), 234.
29. *Jazz Masters in Transition* (New York: Macmillan, 1970; repr. New York: Da Capo Press, 1982), 227.

9. Changes

1. This quotation and the following one are on page 223.
2. "Bitter Hope," 16.
3. "Another View of Coleman," *Down Beat* 27:11(26 May 1960):21.
4. *The Encyclopedia of Jazz in the 60s* (New York: Horizon Press, 1966; repr. New York: Da Capo Press, 1986), 251, 252.
5. Liner notes to *Let Freedom Ring*, Blue Note BST-84106; CDP-46142.
6. James Morgan, Lee's brother, was cited by Michael Cuscuna in the Blue Note newsletter *Blue Notes* (fall 1989): "Although Lee appeared on many records, he really preferred his playing on the *Evolution* album by Grachan Moncur."
7. Quoted in Nat Hentoff's liner notes to *Trompeta Toccata*, Blue Note BST-84181; B21K-84181.
8. "Jazz Lines," *Fanfare* 9:2(Nov.-Dec. 1985):371.
9. Leonard Feather, liner notes to *Judgment*, Blue Note BST-84159.
10. Crouch, "Andrew Hill's Alternative Avant-Garde," 93.
11. A. B. Spellman, liner notes to *Black Fire*, Blue Note BST-84151; BCT-84151.
12. Liner notes to *Smokestack*, Blue Note BST-84160.
13. Liner notes to *Point of Departure*, Blue Note BST-84167.

14. Liner notes to *Spiral*, Arista 1007.
15. Nat Hentoff, liner notes to *Grass Roots*, Blue Note BST-84303.

10. The Last of Hard Bop

1. *Journal of Jazz Studies* 5:2(spring-summer 1979):77.
2. Ibid., 78, 79.
3. "Jazz Lines," 371.
4. "Focus on Freddie Hubbard," *Down Beat* 29:2(18 Jan. 1962):22.
5. "Freddie Hubbard: Talent Reiterated," *The Village Voice* (25 Mar. 1981):47.
6. London: Eyre Methuen Ltd., 1975, 49.
7. *Bird: The Legend of Charlie Parker* (New York: Citadel Press, 1962; repr. New York: Da Capo Press, 1975), 25, 26.
8. Phyl Garland, "Wynton Marsalis: Musical Genius Reaches Top at 21," *Ebony* 38:5(Mar. 1983):32.
9. Unpublished interview with Carlos Figueroa.
10. *In the Moment: Jazz in the 1980s* (New York: Oxford Univ. Press, 1986), 32.
11. Howard Mandel, "Terence Blanchard/Donald Harrison: Young, Gifted, and *Straight Ahead*," *Down Beat* 53:12(Dec. 1986):23.
12. *New York Times*, Arts and Leisure Section (5 Mar. 1989):29.
13. *Rhythm-a-ning*, 267.
14. "Terence Blanchard/Donald Harrison: Young, Gifted, and *Straight Ahead*," 24.
15. Jon Pareles, "Big Ideas Take a Back Seat to a Good Time," *New York Times*, Arts and Leisure Section (6 Dec. 1987):33.
16. Unpublished interview with Carlos Figueroa.

SELECTED HARD BOP
DISCOGRAPHY

This discography includes both recordings discussed in detail and others that the author especially recommends. CD numbers are given after those of the LPs; (op) indicates records currently out of print.

Adderley, Julian "Cannonball." *Jazz Workshop Revisited*. Landmark LLP-1303; LCD-1303-2.

———. *Them Dirty Blues*, Landmark LLP-1301; LCD-1301-2.

Blakey, Art. *At the Café Bohemia-Vol. 2*. Blue Note BST-81508; B21Y-46522.

———. *The Big Beat*. Blue Note BST-84029; B21Y-46400.

———. *New York Scene*. Concord Jazz CJ-256; CCD-4256.

———. *Thermo*. Milestone 47008; *Caravan*. Fantasy OJCCD-038-2; *Ugetsu*. Fantasy OJCCD-090-2.

Brooks, Tina. *The Complete Blue Note Recordings of Tina Brooks*. Mosaic MR4-106.

Brown, Clifford (and Max Roach). *At Basin Street*. Emarcy 814648-2.

———. *Memorial Album*. Blue Note BST-81526; B21Y-81526.

Burrell, Kenny. *Midnight Blue*. Blue Note BST-84123; B21Y-46399.

Byrd, Donald. *Byrd in Hand*. Blue Note BST-84019; B21Y-84019.

Clark, Sonny. *Leapin' and Lopin'*. Blue Note 84091 (op); B21Y-84091.

———. *Max Roach/George Duvivier/Sonny Clark*. Bainbridge 1044; BCD-1044.

Coltrane, John. *Coltrane "Live" at the Village Vanguard*. MCA/Impulse MCAD-39136 (cd only).

———. *Giant Steps*. Atlantic SD-1311; 1311-2.

———. *Impressions*. MCA/Impulse MCA-5887; MCAD-5887.

Davis, Eddie "Lockjaw." *Battle Stations* (with Johnny Griffin). Prestige 7282 (op).
————. *The Cookbook*. 2-Prestige 24039; Fantasy OJCCD-652-2, 653-2.
Davis, Miles. *Bags' Groove*. Fantasy OJC-245; OJCCD-245-2.
————. *Cookin'*. Fantasy OJC-128; OJCCD-128-2.
————. *Dig*. Fantasy OJC-005; OJCCD-005-2.
————. *Elevator to the Scaffold*. Fontana 836305-2 (cd only).
————. *Kind of Blue*. Columbia CJ-40579; CK-40579.
————. *Miles Davis*. Blue Note BST-81501, BST-81502; B21Y-81501, B21Y-81502.
————. *Miles Davis & John Coltrane Live in Stockholm 1960*. Dragon DRLP 90/91; A.V.I. CD-2004.
Dorham, Kenny. *Matador and Inta Somethin'* (with Jackie McLean). Blue Note B2-84460 (cd only).
————. *Quiet Kenny*. Fantasy OJC-250; OJCCD-250-2.
————. *Trompeta Toccata*. Blue Note BST-84181; B21Y-84181.
Ervin, Booker. *Exultation*. Prestige 7844.
Farmer, Art. *Modern Art*. Blue Note B2-84460 (cd only).
————. *Quintet with Gigi Gryce*. Fantasy OJC-241.
Flanagan, Tommy. *The Tommy Flanagan Trio Overseas*. Prestige 7632 (op).
————. *Trinity*. Inner City 1084 (op).
Gillespie, Dizzy. *The Cool World*. Philips 600138 (op).
Green, Bennie (with Eddie "Lockjaw" Davis), J.J. Johnson, Kai Winding. *Trombone by Three*. Fantasy OJC-091.
Griffin, Johnny. *The Little Giant*. Fantasy OJC-136; Riverside JCD-679-1149.
Hancock, Herbie. *The Prisoner*. Blue Note BST-84321; B21Y-46845.
Harris, Barry. *At the Jazz Workshop*. Fantasy OJC-208.
Haynes, Roy and Booker Ervin. *Bad News Blues*. Prestige 2504 (op).
Heath, Jimmy. *Fast Company*. Milestone 47025; *Nice People*. Fantasy OJCCD-6006-2.
————. *Love and Understanding*. Muse MR-5028 (op).
Henderson, Joe. *Inner Urge*. B21Y-84189 (cd only).
————. *Mode for Joe*. Blue Note BST-84227; B21Y-84227.
Hill, Andrew. *Black Fire*. Blue Note BST-84151; B21Y-84151.
————. *Smokestack*. Blue Note BST-84160 (op).
Hope, Elmo. *All Star Sessions*. Milestone 47037; MCD-47037-2.
————. *Trio*. Fantasy OJCCD-477-2 (cd only).
Hubbard, Freddie. *Here to Stay*. Blue Note BST-84135; B21Y-84135.
————. *Ready for Freddie*. Blue Note BST-84085 (op).

Hutcherson, Bobby. *Spiral.* Blue Note LT-996 (op).
———. *Stick-Up!* Blue Note BST-84244 (op).
Jackson, Milt. *Invitation.* Fantasy OJC-260; OJCCD-260-2.
Jazztet (Art Farmer and Benny Golson). *Back to the City.* Contemporary C-14020; JCD-701-14020.
———. *The Jazztet at Birdhouse.* Argo LPS-688 (op).
———. *The Jazztet and John Lewis.* Argo LPS-684 (op).
Jones, Hank. *The Trio.* Savoy MG-12023 (op).
Jordan, Clifford. *The Adventurer.* Muse MR-5163.
Kelly, Wynton. *Full View.* Milestone 9004 (op).
Land, Harold. *The Fox.* Fantasy OJCCD-343-2 (cd only).
McDuff, Jack. *Live!* Prestige 7274 (op).
McLean, Jackie. *Jackie's Bag.* Blue Note BST-84051; B21Y-46142.
———. *Let Freedom Ring.* Blue Note BST-84106; B21Y-46527.
———. *One Step Beyond.* Blue Note BST-84137 (op); B21Y-46821.
Mingus, Charles. *Changes 1 and 2,* Atlantic SD-1677, SD-1678 (op).
———. *Mingus Ah Um.* Columbia CJ-4-0648; CK-40648.
———. *New Tijuana Moods.* Bluebird 5635-1-RB11; 5644-2-RB.
———. *Pithecanthropus Erectus.* Atlantic SD-8809; 8809-2.
Moncur, Grachan, *Evolution.* Blue Note BST-84153; B21Y-84153.
Monk, Thelonious. *Brilliant Corners.* Fantasy OJC-026; OJCCD-026-2.
———. *Monk's Music.* Fantasy OJC-084; OJCCD-084-2.
———. *Thelonious Monk: Genius of Modern Music.* Blue Note BST-81510, 81511; B21Y-81510, 81511.
Montgomery, Wes. *Full House.* Fantasy OJC-106; OJCCD-106-2.
Morgan, Lee. *Here's Lee Morgan.* Vee Jay VJS-3007; Suite Beat SBCD-2008.
———. *The Sidewinder.* Blue Note B11E-84157; B21Y-84157.
———. *Take Twelve.* Prestige 2510; Fantasy OJCCD-310-2.
Newman, David "Fathead." *Still Hard Times.* Muse MR-5283; MCD-5283.
Rollins, Sonny. *On the Outside.* Bluebird 2496-2-RB (cd only).
———. *Plus Four.* Fantasy OJC-243; OJCCD-243-2.
———. *Saxophone Colossus.* Fantasy OJC-291; OJCCD-291.
———. *Worktime.* Fantasy OJC-007; OJCCD-007-2.
Shaw, Woody. *Little Red's Fantasy.* Muse MR-5103.
Shorter, Wayne. *Speak No Evil.* Blue Note BST-84194; B21Y-46509.
Silver, Horace. *The Cape Verdean Blues.* Blue Note BST-84220 (op); B21Y-84220.
———. *Further Explorations.* Blue Note BST-81589 (op).

———. *Horace Silver and the Jazz Messengers.* Blue Note BST-81518; B21Y-46140.

———. *The Tokyo Blues.* Blue Note BST-84110 (op).

Smith, Jimmy. *Home Cookin'.* Blue Note BST-84050 (op).

Turrentine, Stanley. *That's Where It's At.* Blue Note BST-84096; B21Y-84096.

Waldron, Mal. *The Quest.* Fantasy OJC-082.

Weston, Randy. *Randy!* Bakton BRS-1001 (op).

Wilson, Gerald. *On Stage.* Pacific Jazz S-88 (op).

Woods, Jimmy. *Conflict.* Contemporary 7612 (op).

Young, Larry. *Unity.* Blue Note BST-84221; B21Y-84221.

INDEX

Printed in the United States
204307BV00001B/148-159/A